...to run and
not be weary

Bethany

"You're Special"

Jan Cottrell

Phil. 4:13

4/18/90

...to run and not be weary

STAN COTTRELL
Introduction by Ruth Bell Graham

Fleming H. Revell Company
Old Tappan, New Jersey

ALSO BY Stan Cottrell
No Mountain Too High

Unless otherwise identified, Scripture quotations are from the King James Version of the Bible.

Scripture quotations identified NAS are from the New American Standard Bible, © The Lockman Foundation 1960, 1962, 1963, 1968, 1971, 1972, 1973, 1975, 1977.

Excerpt from TIME Magazine Copyright 1984 Time Inc. All rights reserved. Reprinted by permission from TIME.

Library of Congress Cataloging-in-Publication Data

Cottrell, Stan.
  To run and not be weary.

  1. Cottrell, Stan.   2. Runners (Sports)—United
States—Biography.   3. Running—China.   4. China—
Description and travel—1976–   5. Running—
Religious aspects—Christianity. I. Title.
GV1061.15.C66A38   1986   796.4'26 [B]   85-19639

ISBN 0-8007-1444-X

TO those who saw and shared the vision

Carol
Jerry Brentham
Tyler Dixon
Francis Galloway
Mickey Grant
John Hedquist
Percy Helmer
Carl Jones
Anna Kendall
All the students of Dekalb Christian Academy in Atlanta
and Garrett Middle School in Austell, Georgia

TO *Carey Moore, with appreciation for his assistance in the writing of* To Run and Not Be Weary

Contents

Introduction

For one who finds walking down and up our steep driveway an accomplishment, I find running for joy a sheer amazement.

But then Stan Cottrell is a pretty amazing person.

Consider his background, consider his accomplishments, and consider his upcoming goal. He's quite a guy!

You like Stan as soon as you meet him, and it's great that America has such a terrific public relations man. An odd way of doing public relations—but it works!

Having been born and raised in China I was doubly interested in the proposed Friendship Run from the Great Wall in the north to Canton in the south, along side roads.

I read this book with fascination and wondered what the peasants he passed must have thought about Stan. Was he fleeing from something? Was he being punished? Foreigners, they had been told, were always in a hurry. This proved it. Whatever their thoughts, we may never know.

But we are glad three Chinese are coming to run across America with Stan.

May this be just one more step in the growing understanding and friendship between our two great countries.

RUTH BELL GRAHAM

May 1985

Chinese Expressions

Throughout, I have elected to use the modern forms for spelling Chinese words in English. In this *pinyin* system (literally "phonetic spelling") for example, Peking becomes Beijing, Canton becomes Guangzhou, and so on. For easy reference I have listed here some of the more common Chinese expressions found in this book, along with their meanings. The letter *x* and the diphthong *zh* appear frequently in Chinese. They are pronounced as *sh* and *j*, respectively.

Lao pengyo—friend
Ni hau—hello, greetings
Moli hwa cha—jasmine tea
Hun hau—very good
Hun hau chr—very good food
Gungshi—congratulations, a toast from the heart
Gang bei—bottoms up!

Bu gang bei—no bottoms up!
Tai chi—shadow boxing exercise
Meigwo ren—American

All amounts of currency are given in U.S. dollars unless otherwise indicated.

...to run and not be weary

Man is so made that when his soul is on fire with imagination, impossibilities vanish.

　　　　　　　　　—La Fontaine

1

The Journey of Two Thousand Miles

You can talk about a thing for only so long. A woman can carry her baby, but comes a day to deliver. A boxer can boast that he's the greatest, but sounds the bell and he must prove it.

I had talked of running China long enough. Came the day to go out and begin.

I was so jittery that morning that I don't think I would have passed a polygraph test if asked the simplest facts about myself. To counter my nervousness, I tried to mentally shut down the zillion messages my brain was sending me and concentrate on my shaving. But that was about as successful as trying to keep the sun from coming up. In the minute or two it took me to shave, all the time trying to think straight, images flashed before my mind—images of a winding high-

15

way trailing off in the distance, the imposing Great Wall, blue-coated cameramen and women, rugged mountains, Chinese faces laughing, American and Chinese flags unfurling in the wind, speeches. . . .

Another picture flashed on the screen of my mind.

Carol sitting down for Thursday evening supper. Michelle and Stanley III and Jennifer, around the table in the nook, bowing at Carol's words: "Thank You, Jesus. This is the day Daddy's been dreaming of. Thank You for being with him there in China. Let him run well today. Please watch over him, and watch over us. In Your name, Amen."

I patted on some after-shave and thought. *Looking and smelling like a runner won't do it, Stanny boy. You gotta be in shape for what lies ahead of you. You can dress the part, but if you don't have what it takes, you may as well wish after-shave would make you look like Robert Redford.*

The face in the mirror seemed more relaxed than it had in a long while. Lines of strain and worry hadn't vanished, but were less apparent now, more ready to form a natural smile. Of course, the previous night's sixteen-course feast had done nothing to hinder my relaxing and sleeping soundly.

Zhong mei you hao wan cui! Gang bei! Gang bei! they had chanted. *Zhong mei you hao wan cui!* "Long Live Chinese-American friendship!" (I discovered that *zhong* means "center" and this stands for China because the Chinese since ancient times have considered their land as the center of the universe. *Mei* means "beautiful country," their name for America.)

All was quiet now, except for an occasional ring of a bicycler's bell on the Beijing streets below. Pushing aside the bright red curtain I peered out over the awakening Chinese capital to see the gray buildings begin to emerge in the early light. To the north, beyond the belching smokestacks of the city, lay the road where, within hours, I would begin the long run to Guangzhou. It was Friday, October 19, 1984, in the land that gave the world the proverb: "The journey of a thousand miles must begin with a single step." I was eager to take the first step in my journey of two thousand miles.

Slipping on green shorts and a long-sleeved cotton pullover, I sat down on the bed to open a bundle of white cotton socks. I had seen an ad with Runique's promise of blister-free socks and had written and told them that since I had a little running to do, their "no blister" guarantee interested me. They sent me several pair.

Then I pulled on a worn pair of Adidas Oregons. The thought had crossed my mind to start the run in new shoes, but you don't go dancing in new shoes—and you don't go running in them either. In one of my bags I had almost enough shoes to outfit a track team; when I had cleared customs in Beijing, I think the inspector wondered if I were preparing to open a shoe store.

In that room in the Yanjing Hotel I was getting ready to do what I've been doing for seven years—setting out to test the limits of my endurance. Only this time I was attempting it in China.

In 1978 I had run 405 miles across my home state of Georgia. Then came the 24-hour run in Atlanta in 1979, and the Run for America in 1980—3,103.5 miles in 48 days, from New York City to San Francisco. I had done several shorter runs in the South and across my native state of Kentucky, some sponsored by the American Lung Association, and in 1982, The Great European Friendship Run—3,500 miles in 80 days from Edinburgh, Scotland, to the Rock of Gibraltar. Then followed more runs, two in the Dominican Republic and one in Jamaica.

Those last four I considered training runs for this, The Great Friendship Run from China's Great Wall north of Beijing to Guangzhou, 2,125 miles south.

The Great Friendship Run began as an adventure and a challenge, I suppose something like Mount Everest was to Sir Edmund Hillary. Each run had taken me further toward testing my own limits and discovering the kind of inner resources that are lying untapped within. Because the possibility of running across China was there, sooner or later I had to attempt it. Through some quirk of nature—or through God's design, as I prefer to view it—I'm made for running long distances. So, I wanted to run China as a way of glorifying my heavenly Father who has enabled me to do this well. I chose "friendship" as the key because I feel friendship is one of the most precious commodities we can enjoy while on this earth. What a wonderful thing if a run through China could foster friendship between two great nations, and help—in some small way—establish peace. I admit that's a very large dream, but it was seriously a hope to which I clung.

Long before I was ever sure I would do this run, the Salvation Army in Atlanta had presented me with an Army flag, about the size of a man's handkerchief. It was a special one. An astronaut had taken it to the moon. I had worn it in the Dominican Republic and in Jamaica, and now I was wearing it for the first day of the run in mainland China. Its colors are symbolic—red for Christ's shed blood, royal blue for Jesus' pure life, gold for the indwelling Holy Spirit, and fire within the gold representing God's judgment fires, testing man's deeds.

It would be cold on this first day of the run so I also wore warm-up pants and jacket—royal blue with white stripes. My white gloves and blue stocking cap would be handy for later.

The schedule called for breakfast downstairs at 6:00 with Mickey Grant, who would be directing the Chinese camera crew filming the run. We would meet Grace, our Chinese coordinator, at 6:30, leave the hotel at 7:00, and start the run at 8:30 at the Great Wall—if things went according to plan.

Mickey, my lone American companion on this ambitious foray into the Chinese hinterland, is a blond Texan about my height, with ruddy complexion. He had lived in Taiwan three years and, to his considerable credit, could speak Mandarin, albeit with a bit of a drawl I imagine. He and I had met each other in the process of my launching the run, and we were sticking together now like brothers.

Mickey's a borderline Type A personality and thus not one who sits easily in the saddle while nothing's happening— especially when something is supposed to be happening. We met in the hotel lobby at 6:00, with our minds on break-fast, but there, surrounded by our baggage, it was evident that not everything this day would go according to plan. The silence from the hotel kitchen was deafening. Snafu Number 1.

Grace, a staff member of the China Sports Service Company, who would coordinate the run, arrived right on schedule, sized up the situation in a moment, and headed straight for the kitchen. This intelligent young woman with the horn-rimmed glasses is gracious to a marked degree, as her English nickname implies. But diffident she is not when the occasion calls for it. In the lobby we could hear her bark the commands, and minutes later Mickey and I were sitting down to plates of fried eggs, toast, jam, and tea.

On the thirty-mile ride to the Great Wall, eager to begin the run, I couldn't sit still. "I'm going through an interesting set of emotions right now," I told Mickey. Sometimes I would sing—sometimes I would stare out the window.

"I feel like I've been kicked by a mule."

"You're probably not fully recovered from jet lag," Mickey responded. "You had better get to bed early tonight." That didn't appear possible. Tyler Dixon, my business partner, lawyer, and best friend, would be arriving by plane at the Beijing airport that night, bringing with him a critical payment for the China Sports Service Company (a division of the All-China Sports Federation, which is roughly equivalent to the old Amateur Athletic Union in the United States). I wanted to be on hand to meet him.

"I was afraid the banquet last night was going to be stiff and formal," Mickey commented, trying to get my mind off how I was feeling. "But it wasn't that way at all. The Chinese know how to put you at ease." How true. We were two strangers in the midst of a roomful of dignitaries who were speaking a language I could not begin to comprehend, but we had been put at ease from the start.

Grace told us who some of those dignitaries were, as I

watched the flat terrain outside my window. I had taken this ride before, on my first trip to China in December 1983. But I studied the road more carefully now. The plan called for me to begin the run at the Wall, heading south toward Beijing on this same road. Our destination the first day would be the capital; from there we would pick up and proceed into the heartland for what Grace and the heads of China Sports had carefully worked out as a fifty-three-day nonstop journey. By "nonstop" I mean there would be no days off until we reached Guangzhou on December 10.

As we would try to do each day, I read aloud from Oswald Chambers's daily devotional, *My Utmost for His Highest*. My anxiety showed—I chose the reading for October 20 instead of the nineteenth.

Why am I nervous? All I've got to do today is run, and that's what I'm good at. I'd rather do that than almost anything. And now, to be doing it in China after all these years getting here. . . .

A little Chinese boy caught my eye and snapped me out of my introspection as our car sped by, entering mountainous country. For a moment I saw little Stanley Cottrell in that small Chinese lad. I was standing in the cornfield, barely seven years old, with my sister Mary. On that farm in central Kentucky, not far from Munfordville, I had gotten my first taste of running. I so wanted a pet that when I saw a rabbit in our cornfield I chased it until I wore it out. It took hours, but he was now mine. Momma wasn't too encouraging, however, for she knew that "my" rabbit would never last in our backyard where our hound dogs and an old tomcat roamed.

At a county fair at age twelve I won my first honor in racing. It was for the 100-yard dash. I ran in old lace-up work shoes and against Daddy's wishes, because he had no use for running. He wished I could play ball. But I was too little.

I was an average student, but I was an above-average distance runner in our part of the state in high school (but for races of only one and two miles, that's not saying much).

When a twenty-eight-inch snowfall closed the Elizabethtown High School for a month in my senior year, I switched to the school in Cub Run so I could graduate and go to college.

That little runt of a farm boy grew to be obsessed with running. In my senior year, a bunch of my high school classmates bet me five dollars I couldn't run the ten miles from Horse Cave to Munfordville; I took them up on it and ran the whole distance. They forked over five dollars when I reached the Tastee-Freeze at Munfordville, and I treated them all to Cokes.

I entered Western Kentucky University on a partial cross-country scholarship worth sixty dollars—the first Cottrell ever to go to college. I also joined the Marine Corps P.L.C. (Platoon Leader's Class, the marine equivalent of Reserve Officers' Training Corps). But my short-fuse temper exploded one time too many. School fights cost me my chance of becoming an officer. I remember the day I was discharged from the Marine Reserves, I went out and ran for several miles. I was already finding in running a way to cope. When I returned from running, I had a cooler head.

Yet I got myself into another fight at college—this time over a girl—and was asked to drop out for a semester. Fortunately for me, it was time for the Boston Marathon, and I entered that twenty-six-mile event. So far as I know, I was the first Kentuckian to run in the Boston Marathon.

I placed ninety-second that year (1964) though I was sick with a 102-degree temperature. When I got back home and had worked awhile, I reentered Western Kentucky and finished with a degree in physical education and a certificate to teach. First in Michigan and then in Florida, I taught school, and then I went into sales in Georgia, where I first began seeking the broader horizons of long-distance running.

At the Great Wall I put my musing about the past behind me and again felt the "butterflies." I tried to order them to fly in formation, but I wasn't too successful. A lump formed in my throat as I realized that the moment had arrived. But, no, I was still in for quite a wait. It was 8:00 A.M., and there was no sign of the film crew. Snafu Number 2.

The sun climbed into the sky and we waited.

"Okay, so we'll get started a little late," I said to Grace. "We've got to allow for a little confusion until we get used to working together." That was the understatement of the day.

Shielded from the biting cold, our car was parked within a few yards of the Wall. After almost an hour, the Beijing Film Studio vehicles arrived.

My rolling home for the next fifty-three days, a comfortable, Italian-made recreation vehicle belonging to the film studio, had arrived with the film crew. Eager to take a look, I opened the door on the right side of the van and stepped in. No one was inside; I later learned that the RV was off limits to members of the film crew. It was deemed too "comfortable" for them. Most Chinese have never seen RVs; they are unknown there. Because this van appeared to be a place where traveling people would live, the Chinese called it a *da puncha,* a gypsy wagon.

"Italian moviemakers donated this *da puncha* when they finished shooting the Marco Polo television series," Grace said. "The stars used this as their dressing room."

That explained the vanity built into the front wall, complete with lights all along the edge of the large mirror. On either side and across the back wall were cushioned couches below large tinted-glass windows. Blue curtains tied at the corners of the van accented the plain white interior. Overhead were at least six small cabinets. A two-burner gas range filled one corner. The partition gave complete privacy from the driver's compartment.

Like a prospective buyer, I opened a narrow door to discover a closet, and a wider one to find the toilet. *All I will need for my tour through the China interior,* I thought. I wondered how much time I would actually spend there.

Joining the film studio crew at the Wall were photographers from the Associated Press, *Time* magazine, the Xinhua

News (New China News Agency—roughly equivalent to the Associated Press), and others. After they got organized, it was off to the Wall for the prerun publicity shots. I must have run and rerun a stretch of the Wall half a dozen times before all the photographers were satisfied.

The sun continued to climb in the almost cloudless sky and Mickey didn't like what he was seeing. The wind was fierce and the film crew were using heavy "body pod" or hand-held (in popular parlance) cameras. He knew that they could not hold them steady in that wind and film a moving target.

"Hey, stop," he cried. "Get those cameras on tripods."

"But we didn't bring a tripod," they answered. To our consternation, one of them explained that there wasn't enough money for a tripod! That proved not quite true, for Mickey later found out that the camera operators had tripods in the trucks, but they had not brought them because the guard at the entry gate to the Wall required a five-dollar fee. And members of the film crew didn't have five dollars in their pockets to spend on a tripod. Snafu Number 3.

Nothing so eloquently revealed the doubts that still lingered in some minds concerning The Great Friendship Run as did that one little reluctance by the film studio to pay that fee. True, the check for the studio's first payment would not arrive until Tyler came late that night. But we had already paid $30,000 to China Sports and I thought that demonstrated enough reliability to be trusted for pocket-change expenses.

While Mickey attacked that problem, I was temporarily distracted by the arrival of American army officers, including a one-star and a two-star general. Some of them came over to talk, telling me they had heard about The Great Friendship Run, and wishing me well. When we learned the following day that they were in Beijing for secret China-United States air maneuvers, we felt included in a tiny bit of international intrigue.

Frozen and frustrated, I went to the *da puncha* and sipped hot tea with Grace. The sun was climbing yet higher in the sky and I was eager to run. But the Chinese were insisting on propriety. There would have to be a ceremony befitting such an auspicious occasion as The Great Friendship Run.

"It's time," Grace finally said, and motioned to me to go to the road where people had gathered. *"Shao huhu!"* she said. I laughed. This is what she had said to me on our very first visit to the Wall, when I got out and ran on the Wall, all bundled up against the cold. A loose translation is, "You have a good heart, but you are stupid!" Grace laughed too, good naturedly. She was almost as glad as I that we were getting started.

Over the roadway they had stretched a colorful banner, announcing in Chinese and English, "The Great Friendship Run." It billowed and snapped in the wind, which also threatened to knock over the loudspeakers. To a gathering of a hundred or so dignitaries, Sports Service staff, camera people, newsmen, and tourists, Mr. Wang, the vice-president of China Sports Service Company, gave a brief speech and then motioned to me to come to the mike.

"I am very glad to be here," I said, my heart pumping the adrenaline through my system. "And I thank your government and all of the people of the United States of America who have made this run possible. I come in the spirit of friendship. Thank you for opening the doors of Chinese hospitality and friendship to me."

I had brought with me a Georgia flag that had flown over the state capitol—a symbol of the American people and what I hoped to achieve by this run—and I presented it to Mr. Wang. Then, with a wave to the people, I walked nervously to the starting point beneath the banners. We were finally ready.

The people quieted as an official raised a small gun to the sky. For a few seconds the wind died and a perfect stillness prevailed.

Bang!

My watched showed 10:54 A.M. Not quite on schedule, but I was off and running.

Boy, oh, boy. The torrent of thoughts that came to me

would have made me a top contender for the Bette Davis award for drama. Vicariously I could identify with Neil Armstrong in his words: "That's one small step for a man; one giant leap for mankind." I was taking the first official steps in the long journey to Guangzhou and daring to dream that by doing so the distance between China and the good ol' USA would not be so great.

2

Which Way to China?

I can't fix the date exactly when I first thought of running in China—it was sometime in May 1980—but I'll never forget the circumstances. An attorney had called me to his office to meet a big-time promoter, Don Studley.

Don was just what I had heard he was—big time. But not for sports events. He promoted rock groups. Here he stood, sunglasses pushed up into his brown hair, shirt buttoned halfway, gold chains around his neck, jeans flared at the bottom, leather boots. I mean Cool! He started talking about this "gig" across the United States—his term for my forthcoming run from New York City to San Francisco.

"We need eight girls, shapely, in eye-catching outfits going ahead of you into towns, handing out American flags. . . ."

I tried to keep a straight face, but I was thinking,

You can't do this like Sonny and Cher, or Andy Gibb, or the dozen other celebrities you've worked with.

He kept talking. "Now after this gig, what can you do for an encore?" He paused. Then his eyes brightened. "That's it, baby. There's nothing unless you do something really crazy like run the China Wall!"

Don and I never did work together, but what he said that day connected with something deep within me. *Why not?* I thought. *Why not run the Great Wall?* Mentally I drew a circle in the air and wrote in: CHINA. *That's it! That will solidify my name and ability. People will know me. I will run the China Wall.*

That summer my priorities were all wrong. I was on a gigantic ego trip, living for I, me, and mine. All I could see was what the Run for America would bring me in fame and funds. At the time my running achievements were bringing me frequent speaking engagements at sales meetings (frequently for free!) and before high school audiences. I didn't beat around the bush. I told everyone who would listen that success went to the fellow who hung on five minutes longer. "There's no mountain too high, no valley too low, no road too long."

I would throw in a few homespun Kentucky specials I learned from my dad, like "You can't look at a bullfrog's hind end and tell how far it can jump." Oh, my. Talk came easy. I could stand up and spout off a lot of sound and fury about goal setting and "hanging in there." But little did I realize that I was about to have more than ample opportunity to find out whether I believed enough in what I was saying to stake my life on it. I was about to arrive at that proverbial crossroads of Put Up or Shut Up.

In August 1980, a month after completing the run across America, my phone was not bringing the world to my door as I had hoped. Studley and other potential promoters had faded out of my plans about as quickly as they had come in, and I was looking for a way to run on the Great Wall of China. I called New York City to introduce myself to an export-import company doing business in China. I was like an old blind hog rooting for an acorn. If he keeps rooting long enough, he'll turn up something.

I knew about as much about China as a hog knows about a prayer meeting. Peking, the Great Wall, and Hong Kong was all I knew about the world's most populous nation, and I didn't even realize that Hong Kong is a British Crown Colony (China would be offended by that!).

I astounded the man I contacted when I told him of my dream (I spoke of it as a plan) to run the Great Wall. His amazement telegraphed to me over the phone and I'm sure he thought I was not quite all there—about three bricks short of a full load. But since a television engagement was bringing me to New York, he invited me to drop in.

On the basis of a few hours' discussion that was sometimes a little over my head—talk of things like media value, impressions, and exposure—we struck a deal.

"We'll handle everything, kiddo," they told me. "You just run. We'll get the sponsors. This run should gross $5 million plus."

My cut would be 40 percent—of $5 million! Well, that can buy a lot of beans and taters and allow for lots of gooseberry pie on Sundays. I thought, *Stanley junior, this is no time to get greedy. But go for it!* I returned to Georgia to await their call, secretly telling myself, *I'll run the Great Wall and that will pave the way to making my fortune.*

A month went by. Two months went by. My dream was growing by the minute and I began opening my big mouth. "I'll run on the Great Wall in China in the spring of 1981," I boasted.

It turned out that my New York connection belonged to the school of "It can't be done." I've learned that when someone starts with negative talk, it's like a thread breaking in a sweater. The garment begins to unravel little by little. This company played charades with me for almost a year while I kept thinking, *Any day now.* The only positive thing they did for me was spare me the pain of knowing the initial reaction of the Chinese to my idea of running the Great Wall. Later I learned that when a committee in China first heard of my dream, one man in the meeting actually laughed so hard at the idea that he fell out of his chair. I was Mr. Naive about China, but I wasn't about to give up.

While hoping that this firm would come through for me, I kept "fishing," calling anyone who remotely knew someone with a connection to China. Then one day I heard from New York. They had hit a slight snag—called the Great Wall. Some official had told them that a feasibility study would be necessary to determine if the Wall was runnable. The feasibility study would take six months and cost $200,000.

"And we don't judge that's feasible," my agent said. "We don't know of anyone who would put up that kind of money, just for a study!"

Who was I to argue? The run looked impossible, "infeasible," because of a giant snag.

Eight or nine months passed—months when at times I wondered if my dream were too visionary. Yet the dream wouldn't die. I went out and bought a large map of China and began getting familiar with the land, its history, and its people.

More than anything I was intrigued by the Wall, the longest man-made structure on earth and the only one visible from outer space. I read that the ancient Chinese built the Great Wall over a period of almost two thousand years, beginning in the third century B.C. I also learned something that forced me to relinquish my obsession with running the Wall. Much of its fifteen hundred miles is in ruins and sections are separated by gaping breaks hundreds of feet long.

So, I couldn't run on the Wall, I concluded. But I could run across China, on the existing roads. I was convinced of that. Reading about China, I wanted to meet the Chinese. My dreams sought wings again, and every time I thought of reestablishing contact with China, I thought of New York; if a contact was to be found, that's where I would have to find it, I figured. But I was wrong.

In March 1981 one of the commissioners of our local

thought there was a hurdle—and falling on my face. One day Tyler would not talk deals any longer.

"Stan," he said, his blue eyes seeking to reach inside and arrest my full attention. "I'm convinced that nothing you do is going to succeed until you get your life right with God."

"What?"

I was furious. This I didn't need. But I knew that Tyler could not be put off. He's fireplug and bulldog combined; when his mind is made up, he won't budge and he'll eat you alive. He sat there insisting that my priorities had to change.

I continued trying to do things my way. That's human nature, I guess. But I was getting nowhere. I ran every day, training for some local events coming up. But even my daily runs brought me no peace. I could not run away from myself. Finally, one day while I was running, I left the road and ran to a wooded area; and there I collapsed on my knees.

"Oh, God," I cried. "Oh, God."

Tyler's intransigence had only brought everything else to a head. Carol and I had grown distant. My quiet, brown-haired wife kept trying to tell me that I didn't need to be forever trying to impress people. "Stan," she would say, "people will like you just because of you, not because you run. That's merely incidental."

I took her criticism to mean that she didn't understand me, and that she didn't really care how much running meant to me. Yet I knew she was right. I was an accomplishoholic. I would volunteer for everything and strive for every kind of award possible. Then I would say to myself, in the words of the Peggy Lee hit, "Is that all there is?"

Things had gotten so bad that I had thought seriously of walking out on my family and going to some other state and starting over. The kids were smaller then: Michelle was thirteen, Stanley III was twelve, and Jennifer was six. I couldn't find a job and wasn't earning any money. I felt useless. But I couldn't even run away. The family station wagon that was to be the "escape vehicle" had burned to an empty hull beside a highway several days earlier.

"Oh, God," I cried. "I hate myself and I hate life. If there's anything You can salvage, You can have it. . . ."

That was the turning point.

Gobbler's Knob, Kentucky, was baby Stan's first home
Near Needmo, No Hope, Black Gnat, Zero, Devil's Backbone
They never had much money, life was hard and seldom fun
Stan Junior was too small for ball, but big enough to run!

Stan Cottrell is a runner, He's run for thirty years
He's run in pain, He's run in rain,
    through snow and bitter tears
He's run in heat that melts the street,
    his critics think him odd
He doesn't run for you or me, Stan Cottrell runs for God

Stan ran 'cross the U.S.A., through Europe, China, too
He'd go 'round the world in eighty days,
    just 'tween me and you
He's a world record setter who keeps gettin' better,
    man, ol' Stan can run
Tho' far from home, Stan's never alone,
    thanks to God's only Son . . .

Stan's been down the road and back,
    he's been on the valley floor
He's asked himself more than once,
    "What am I doing this for?"
He's stared up at the mountain peaks silhouetted
    against the sky
And longed for wings of eagles that he might
    mount up and fly

There was a time he ran for glory, a time he ran
    for fame
His heart's desire was no higher than that
    people know his name
But Stan ran into trouble, and Stan fell on his face
'Til he reached out and took God's hand,
    Stan was running in one place.

A man can run from trouble, a man can run from life
A man can run away from home, from his children,
  from his wife
But a man can't run forever, he can't put life
  up on a shelf
A man can't run to God's own Son 'til he runs
  out of himself*

---

* "Stan Cottrell Runs for God" by Tom Taylor. Copyright 1985—Thomas A. Bryan Taylor. Used by permission.

3

From Gobbler's Knob to Beijing

When Tyler saw me coming to tell him about Percy Helmer, he could just hear my cheer:

"Percy, Percy, he's our man, if he can't do it, somebody else can!"

Tyler knew Percy and respected his business ability. Also, Tyler noticed that I was different. I had a peace I had not possessed before. What had happened on my knees that day had made a difference. Now I found myself 'splaining things to God, and I thought I heard Him say:

> Son, I'm not going to say no to you. But first I'm going to have to grow you up. I can't let a child go to China. I need a man to do that—it's menfolks' work. I'm not saying

no, but it's going to be a slow process until
I get you where I can trust you to go to
China.

Percy was both an enthusiast and an energizer. His excitement, over the least possibility, sent my hopes soaring.

By late 1981 he opened contact with the China Sports Service Company through one of his representatives, a former police chief of Shanghai. Another representative, Andrew Tsung, a renowned Chinese architect, opened doors that had been impossible for Percy or me. "Andy" understood China from his educational background and believed in the dream of friendship between our countries. Word came back that this project had gone all the way up the ladder to the Central Committee in China.

"Now the Chinese want to know how the American government feels about this," Percy told me. "You must meet at least two of five conditions." I was learning that dealing with the Chinese is like climbing two ladders. They will take a step and then they expect you to take an equivalent one.

The conditions were: a letter from President Reagan or former President Carter, a letter from Vice-President Bush, a letter from the U. S. State Department, and the endorsement of a senator and a congressman.

The only politician I ever knew personally was the county judge back in Munfordville, and he had died several years earlier. I didn't know how to begin. But Granny Cottrell used to have a saying: "When e'er a task is set before you, do not idle sit or view it, or be content to wish it done, just begin at once, and do it!"

I figured that a letter from Jimmy Carter would be easy to obtain, since he lived in my home state. But I was wrong. His would be among the last to come in. I went to work phoning congressmen and writing the White House, but I was getting nowhere. So, Tyler and I flew to Washington to knock on doors.

For the most part, we were received warmly wherever we went. Senator Walter Huddleston of Kentucky sponsored a

Senate resolution commending the run. Wyche Fowler, Jr., a congressman from Georgia, fostered a similar one in Congress. And Senator Howard Baker of Tennessee read an endorsement into the *Congressional Record*.

Back in the hotel room, Tyler and I laughed at the comments we had heard that day. "Everyone is talking of the plight of the runner," one told us. "You are the talk of all political Washington," someone else had said. We stayed on for two more days, meeting many caring, sympathetic people on Capitol Hill who went out of their way to make the China run a reality. In a short while we had obtained a letter of endorsement from the State Department plus strong personal letters from fifty senators and congressmen. Then we flew home.

We couldn't help feeling pretty puffed up, and when our wives met us at the Atlanta airport, they seemed pretty smug also. After we spouted out all of our good news, Carol showed us a letter that had come from Vice-President Bush, wishing us well and endorsing the run. To this day we don't know how he was contacted.

Three of the five conditions had been met. And months later a fourth one would also be met—with the aid of former Budget Director Burt Lance I received a personal letter from Jimmy Carter.

Everything for the moment looked bright. When Mr. Tsung delivered the endorsements word came back favorably. The run was on; invitations would be forthcoming and Vice-Premier Yang would receive us with a banquet in the Great Hall of the People. Tyler and I immediately began planning a trip to Beijing for March.

One night in the first week of March, Ted Koppel reported on "Nightline" that the Chinese were "infuriated" by our government's decision to sell arms to Taiwan. Some of our friends were concerned about how this might affect the run, but I assured them that it would have no effect at all.

"You wait and see. We're goin' to China!" I'm never negative, but I could have been a little more realistic!

On the first Sunday in March, Percy called. He had received a telex from Beijing. I couldn't wait to hear, for I was sure that this would be our ticket to China.

"Stan, it's not good," he said. I went numb as he read the words.

> *After consideration, we find it difficult to hold the run. Please understand us. We treasure the friendship between the Chinese people and the American people for which we wish to make efforts. We wish to contact you when condition permits of it. (Signed, China Sports Service.)*

Percy said a few other things; I don't remember what. That day Tyler and I were taking our families out to celebrate our forthcoming venture. Carol and I took the family to church, but I was walking around in a daze. I never heard a word of the sermon. Only Carol knew what had happened, and she shared my shock.

At lunch Tyler and Dee Dee asked, "Have you two had a fight? Has someone died?" I handed Tyler the telex, and started crying, sputtering out the words, ". . . I refuse to give up on this. I know God has a very special reason for saying no right now. . . ."

Almost three years of work had gone down the drain. My heart pounded so that I thought it would rip my chest cavity wide open.

That next day telexes zinged back to China, searching for some explanation. Tyler wrote to the State Department, which we had kept apprised of progress on the run, forwarding more endorsements to the China Affairs Office and asking for some show of government backing that we could present to the Chinese.

On March 23, the Director of China Affairs wrote: "We appreciate your keeping us in touch re your negotiations. . . . I hope that conditions will permit your ambitious effort to proceed. We remain interested in and encourage people-to-people exchanges such as The Great Friendship Run."

In time we learned that our government's agreement to sell military-aircraft parts to Taiwan had caused the political winds to blow cold. And we had been caught in the draft. The perennial optimist, I was glad at least that China had only postponed the run.

All the while, I had been seriously training, running more than a hundred miles a week. I was primed for another big run, ready to burst out of the runner's blocks—but suddenly I was in a holding pattern.

Training for China, I had become acquainted with Hugo Greiner, a doctor whose specialty is sports medicine. He lived a few miles away and unselfishly began helping me with my training diet and offering to monitor my body weight and biochemical functions so that I could continue to challenge the limits. One day we were talking and for the umpteenth time I expressed my disappointment over China.

"Well, Stanny boy, there's always Europe," he said. "Why don't you run Europe? You certainly don't have to go through all this hassle to run over there."

"Why not?" I answered Hugo. And that became Day One in the strategy for my eighty-day run through twelve countries of Europe in the fall of '82. Hugo went with me as my personal physician and coach, and the Fortune Group, an Atlanta-based management training company, sponsored us.

"In the meantime, I can still work on China," I continued. "Maybe the publicity from a Europe run would convince the Chinese that I'm for real."

So I concentrated on training for the European Friendship Run, raising funds for it, and assembling a support team. In August, two months before that run was to begin, China was definitely on the "back burner"—I had little time to contemplate it. But Percy continued knocking on the door for me. And a number of different people wrote to me, or came to see me, offering their assistance. One day a letter arrived from Beijing:

> I think your coming (to China) will be the best thing that could happen to our two countries at this time . . . I am willing to do everything to make . . . the run a reality. (Signed, B/Gen. Bernard Loeffke)

The words sent my spirits soaring. General Loeffke was the defense attaché assigned to the United States embassy in

China's capital. A professor from West Georgia College, while visiting in Beijing, had made a "cold" call on General Loeffke and explained my dilemma to him. The general's letter and our friendship developed as a result. A very key cold call, to say the least.

We had learned by then that the Chinese would not consider a run of the length I was requesting except in the spring or fall. From January to April the temperatures are too cold. And summer is the busy farming season when all roads would be jammed with people hauling goods to market. The earliest date for my run, we concluded, would be September 1983, and that became our next goal.

My emotions, so high after General Loeffke's words, bottomed out when Percy received the following message from Beijing:

Do not contact us. We will contact you.

There was nothing happening, and nothing we could do. Yet I couldn't quit. My daddy had drilled that into me. When I was a boy, Daddy used to wrestle with my brother Harold and me. He would get me down, pull my arm up behind me, and hold it until it started to hurt, and then say, "Do you 'mit? Do you 'mit?" And if I said yes, Daddy would answer, "No, you can't, 'cause Cottrells never 'mit!" (Cottrells never submit.)

I remember Daddy getting a hammerlock on Harold and holding it for thirty or forty minutes. All of the time Harold would be screaming and crying.

"Do you 'mit?" Daddy would ask him.

"No!" Harold would holler, even though he thought he was going to die.

"Why?" Daddy would ask.

" 'Cause Cottrells never 'mit!"

Finally Daddy would let him go. This happened over and over while we were growing up. We had sore arms for a week after one of those encounters with Daddy. But one thing stuck in our souls—Cottrells never 'mit.

I was right on the verge of quitting now. It didn't help

things that people seemed to be taking me for a screwball, a goofball, an eccentric man obsessed with China, someone who couldn't make up his mind what he was going to do. I had run in Europe while "training for China." I had gone to the Dominican Republic for the first of two runs there—in my mind, more "training for China." But I wondered—*Will I ever get my chance?*

I avoided people who knew me, because inevitably someone would ask, "When's the new date?"

"Lord," I prayed. "Are You trying to tell me something? Am I blind? Do I not have my listener on . . . ?

"I give up. If You want me to run in China, You're going to have to make it happen. I can't."

The chickens had come home to roost. Did I believe in my dream or didn't I? Echoing through my mind were the words I had said to others: *Never give up. Never give up. It sounds easy, but it may require everything you've got. . . .*

How well I knew! Prayer eased my emotions that day, but I did not know how this impasse could be overcome—or if it could.

Three days later Ara Kalpak called. He asked: "Hey, bud, what's going on with China?" Ara's not an ordinary friend. He's an achiever, the kind of person you want to listen to when he speaks, because you know he will have something significant to say.

Ara drew from me the essential facts that nothing at all was "going on with China," and then said, "There's a friend of mine here who I want you to meet. . . ." I thought I was hearing a recording.

The next day Ara introduced me to Myron Gray, a nice guy, a mere kid, twenty-two years old. He and I talked a good while. Myron was idealistic, I reasoned. He had not been dipped in the acid bath of reality. What could he do for me?

"It is interesting," I said, trying to find some good in this litle chat. "Three days ago I told God that if He wanted this run to happen, He was going to have to do it. And now you come along."

"I've got a friend who lived in Hong Kong and who has quite a few contacts with those in the Chinese upper echelon," Myron told me. "If you can give me some papers that tell about you, I would be glad to send them to my friend. I think he could help you."

I agreed to give him something, but meanwhile I took on the role of the sage and began trying to give him some wise counsel. He was about to graduate from college and he would have to find out about the "real world." In that "real world" former President Jimmy Carter and Vice-President Bush, senators and congressmen, governors and other dignitaries, had endorsed the run in China. Congressional resolutions were on record in favor of The Great Friendship Run. But to no avail. What could this stranger do?

But young Myron continued to talk glowingly of his friend in Pittsburgh. He exuded the sort of boyish enthusiasm and "can do" optimism that I usually relish.

Then came the kicker.

His friend would need a check for fifty dollars.

"What kind of friend is he?" I asked.

Myron didn't flinch. "Well, if he's going to make some phone calls to China, I think you ought to put up some money to cover that."

I honestly did not have fifty dollars to spare, but I reluctantly agreed to go that far.

Afterward, in talking to Ara, I voiced my skepticism about what this contact of Myron's could do for me. He was hopeful, but I figured that this would go nowhere. I wished I could be as optimistic as Ara.

"Maybe—we'll see," I told him.

A week later Myron's friend called.

"Stan," he said, his strong voice telegraphing confidence. "This is Howard Donnelley. Myron Gray sent me a package containing your communications with China. Here's what's wrong. In your proposal you're using complicated language. Words like *pursuant* have got to go. It has to be simple. No more than five sentences. When you've got it written out, send it to me."

That same day, the new, simple, five-sentence proposal for The Great Friendship Run was in the mail to Mr. Donnelley. Then I waited to see what this voice on the other end of the line could do.

In three days, on October 20, a telex arrived from China:

From Mr. Howard Donnelley we understand you would like to come to China for discussions about friendship long run by yourself. We welcome you to Beijing, December 1–20. (Signed, China Sports Service)

On its face, the message sounded as though China Sports Service had just heard of me for the first time. But I wasn't going to complain. It was finally time to pack my bags for Beijing.

Howard wrote to account for his use of my fifty dollars— "four telexes and three calls"—adding:

Note, they have OK'd Beijing to Guangzhou. This means the event is on. You must send in an official application to Mr. Kong, a very good and old friend of mine. Let me see it before you send it. . . . In your proposal you must tell them more clearly that you will pay expenses, whatever they are. They must not understand this at this point.

A letter to Howard dated October 21 revealed that all of our earlier negotiations had not gone for naught. China Sports Service wrote that they had "been informed of it through other channels." Howard's "good and old friend," Kong Qingwen, would be in charge of the run; other branches of the Chinese government were requesting information. We were later to be informed that the key points of our discussions with China Sports Service were "subject to approval by highest authority."

Concluding with a note that more money would be needed for the advance work on the run (since I would be running through five provinces), it said:

Now we are making contacts with concerned departments. Thank you very much for your good will and gracious concerns and sincerity to us. This shows that the friendship and cooperation between us is developing daily and we will do our best to make it a success.

"Okay, pal, you've got a 'go' situation," Howard said when he called me the next day. They have committed and when they do that, they won't turn back."

I wanted to meet this man who had done so much for me, and as it would happen, I was flying to Pittsburgh that week on business. He agreed to see me and we made an appointment—to meet at an ice cream parlor, of all places. I was used to meeting important people in their office, but that wasn't Howard's style. He doesn't care for appearances. The person matched the voice: he was tall, a striking figure, with a manner that commanded respect. We talked for an hour.

"Stan," he said, "you will do just fine with the Chinese. Be just like you are with me. . . . Be the 'good ol' boy' you are. You're going to be just fine."

Flying home to Atlanta, I wondered how I was going to scrape the money together for a ticket to China. I couldn't have bought the whistle off a steamboat if they had been selling for a nickel a dozen.

Some businessmen who had watched me persist in this goal of running China were beginning to say things like: "This character is actually going to pull this thing off with the Chinese." They viewed my dream more seriously. And on the day before I was to fly to China, one of them arranged a round-trip ticket for me to Beijing.

4

Crazy American!

Mr. Kong Qingwen and Miss Huang Yayan rode with me in the rear seat of the black vehicle that took me from the airport to the hotel the night I arrived in Beijing. I was to learn that the proper name for the kind of car we were riding in is "Shanghai car"—a sedan with silk curtains at the side and rear windows. Virtually every car I saw in China was equipped with the window curtains.

I guessed Mr. Kong was a few years younger than my forty. He was direct, businesslike, firm yet friendly, of muscular build as befitting his responsibilities with the China Sports Service Company. He stood about my own height as did his female assistant. Of a thinner build, and about the same age as Mr. Kong, Miss Huang wore slacks and a simple white blouse under her light brown jacket. When I attempted to pronounce her name, she smiled—it seemed she was always smiling.

"You can call me Grace," she said, putting the tip of her left middle finger on her black horn-rimmed glasses and pushing them slightly upward.

"That's a beautiful name. We hear it often in the United States. It has a special meaning."

"I know," she replied, "I have an aunt who is a Christian and she told me one time the meaning."

Grace proved to be as gracious as her name.

To be in the People's Republic—in "Communist China"—and already to be reminded of God's grace went a long way toward making me feel at ease. I could not believe that finally I was in the land of my four-year-long dream. It was a strange, new world. Here I was, riding through the darkened streets of the renowned capital of the People's Republic. Outside the car window I could see occasional donkey carts drawing drowsy passengers wrapped against the bitter December cold, while inside, friendly talk erased my apprehensions and prepared me for the night's rest I needed.

My room that first night was small and plain, but quite adequate. They were housing me in a hotel where China Sports has accommodations for visiting athletes. I saw few faces that night, and during my five-day stay I did not see another American face.

Exhausted from the twenty-five-hour flight, I collapsed into bed. The last thing Mr. Kong had said before bidding me good night was that we would meet for a talk in my room at 9:30 the following morning.

On the edges of my mind the anxieties about what lay ahead gnawed away. Tyler and I had been apprehensive about my coming by myself to have these discussions. But the telex had made it plain—I was to come alone. On the flight over, I had wondered what I was getting myself into.

"The Chinese can be tough negotiators," Howard had warned. I would soon learn.

Sleep came easily, but not for long. My body was ready for a long winter's nap, but my mind was running ahead to tomorrow. Lying awake in the middle of my first night in China, I couldn't resist the temptation to sneak a peek at the sleeping city. At my window I stood for a long enchanted moment. Outside I could only make out the indistinct images of buildings, and a deserted street below.

I can't believe I'm actually in Communist China, I told myself. *It's like I'm living on another planet.*

Again I dropped into bed and tried to sleep, but my mind was watching reruns of the long road I had taken to this point.

Sometime in the wee hours I went again to the window, but it was still too dark to see anything. I wondered if the room was bugged, and couldn't resist peeking behind pictures and under the nightstand for hidden microphones. I felt stupid, as though in a James Bond movie, and laughed at myself.

The ceiling in the hotel room must have been fourteen feet high. I went to the bathroom and turned on the light. Above the mirror was a small door, slightly ajar, and I wondered if someone might be hiding there to observe me. It was too high for me to reach, so I brought a chair into the bathroom to stand on so I could see into this storage area. Nothing was there.

After another attempt at sleep, I returned to the window. I pressed my nose against the glass and my breath quickly fogged the window. In the moisture, I wrote: China. And I laughed.

I stood apart, looking on my amazing new world. All about me was an eerie silence, as if all humanity had vanished and I was the only one left.

What are you doing here? I asked myself. I seemed strangely out of place.

Slowly the day dawned, drawing back the curtain on the city as it awakened. The first movement I remember was that of a lone bicycler. Gradually, buildings loomed into view. I counted ninety-seven as far as I could see, gray monoliths against a leaden sky. From every chimney, the black smoke of coal furnaces belched into the air. I was beginning to understand why so many of the people whom I had seen the night before wore masks. The pollution in Beijing surprised me and served to remind me that it hasn't been too many years since the cities in America and industrial Europe languished under coal dust and soot.

Below me now the trickle of bicycles soon became a sea of humanity. Here and there, on the sidewalks and porches, a few citizens were doing their *tai chi*. Before then I had only seen this rhythmical shadowboxing in movies and on television.

What's this? Could it be a giant caterpillar winding its way down the street? I laughed aloud at my first impression of Beijing's double-section buses, which bend like accordions. Later in the day I would observe a "normal" load in these vehicles—people jammed in and hanging out the windows. In this metropolis of 8 million people, few own a car, so the buses have to carry everyone who is going beyond the normal distance traveled on bike.

Standing at that window I kept thinking: *Every evening in Georgia as we get ready for bed, this sea of people is pedaling its way to work.* I thought of how small America seemed compared with China and the rest of the world, and I felt insignificant and incredibly lonely—far, far from home.

The view shocked the senses; I grope for adjectives to describe how I felt that morning. *Gloom* is the most fitting word, I think. I hoped that my further impressions would be more positive.

I found out that the Chinese value punctuality. In my first experiences, when a meeting was called for eight o'clock, they would be there at eight—not a minute before—or after. Later I would learn that in this regard the Chinese are human like the rest of us, and that there is even a fair amount of "mañana" in the Chinese approach to things.

Evidently, the Chinese way—once one arrives for an appointment—is also to go right in and not to knock, for promptly at the agreed-upon hour, in walked Mr. Kong and Grace.

Thanks to Howard, I knew it was also the Chinese way to go casual. "Don't wear a business suit," he had instructed me, and I was glad I had not. Both Mr. Kong and Grace wore shirts and slacks. If we were to experience barriers, it would not be due to clothing.

Mr. Kong got immediately to business. He and Grace sat opposite me. A low table, on which stood the customary thermos of hot water for tea, was between us. In a while we were joined by Mr. Cui (pronounced Swee), a gentle spirit whom I would grow to like very much.

For an hour we discussed the run. I would begin at the Great Wall, thirty miles north of Beijing, and run a total of fifty-one days to Guangzhou in the south. Beijing is situated near the fortieth parallel and Guangzhou is almost squarely on the Tropic of Cancer, so the distance would be like running from Philadelphia to Havana, or from Denver to Mazatlán. The prospective itinerary would take me through five provinces: Hebei, Henan, Hubei, Hunan, and Guangdong.

The China Sports Service Company would provide accommodations through its staff in each province, as well as security, vehicles, meals, and a support crew, which would include a doctor or nurse should I need their services. Xinhua News would cover the event, with media representatives from the foreign press permitted at the start and the finish.

The critical point that day was to agree to pay China Sports a total of $95,000 for the run. A portion of the sum would go to the agent of the company in each province, based on the number of days I would be running through that particular province.

I felt Mr. Kong was being fair with me, and we reached an agreement as he had said, "without difficulty."

"Lunch will be at twelve noon," this cordial host said as we finished. "Perhaps you want to freshen up."

Howard had told me that a contract would not be issued right away, and that was exactly how it turned out. Since I was the one requesting permission for the run, it now fell to me to draft a memorandum of agreement and submit it to Mr. Kong, which I did while I was in Beijing. He had it translated into Chinese, and I felt we were on our way to a contract.

"Blessed is he who knows nothing for he shall find everything amazing." On my second full day in China I witnessed a phenomenon that would qualify as truly amazing in anyone's vocabulary. For me, it was a mighty big step toward my ultimate dream of running China. I went to the Wall.

What will it be like? I asked myself. Here I was in China, not quite able to absorb all of the sights and sounds and smells I was encountering—like a child seeing Disneyland. I had read of the Great Wall's ancient origin. Begun during the Ch'in dynasty in the third century B.C., when the Roman Empire was still a vision waiting fulfillment, lengthy sections have been constructed and added in the twenty-three centuries since then. Its present form can be dated to the seventeenth century, the last days of the Ming dynasty.

I knew that the Wall winds and stretches some fifteen hundred miles east and west along the southern border of the Mongolian plain and that it was intended as a bulwark against invading warriors. What if the Great Wall could be transformed into a symbol of the friendship of neighboring nations and all peoples? I wanted The Great Friendship Run to foster that idea; to tear down walls between our two countries; to help bring cultures together instead of keeping them apart.

Someone has called the Wall "the world's longest graveyard," because many laborers gave their lives in building it, and their bodies lie entombed beneath its stones. The Chinese believe the stones contain the spirits of their ancestors.

As the driver sped northward that afternoon, December 3, I strained to catch my first glimpse of the Wall. Grace and I were warm in the backseat of the Shanghai car, but the people on the road were bundled up against the frigid air. Many of them wore the surgical masks so common in the Orient.

As the plains gave way to mountainous terrain, I grew more anxious. Then suddenly there it was, in the distance, the Great Wall draped on the undulating landscape like a huge slumbering serpent.

"Unreal! Awesome! Incredible!" was all I could say as we came closer.

Grace had pointed out to me that the part of the Wall we would see had been restored since 1949 and that millions of tourists had viewed it. Still, to me, it was breathtaking. From the mountainside, it rises an average 25 feet in height and is 22 feet thick at the base, 19 feet wide on top. At every 200 meters along its crenulated length stands a sentry tower.

With my running shoes on and swathed in a bulky army coat, I left Grace and the driver and hurried up onto the Wall. Few people were out, as the cold weather had closed in on us. But with light heart, I took off running. I couldn't believe it. I was actually running on the Great Wall.

I must have run a mile, my heart full as I lifted one foot after the other. At places the grade is steep, probably forty-five degrees.

My face was freezing, but I didn't care. I just wanted to savor the moment. Before I turned to run back to where I had started, I stopped and ran my hand over individual stones and tried to imagine the person who had laid that stone. Each one had its own story. I was on the Wall for close to an hour before returning to find Grace in the car.

When I got in she laughed and said, "I think you are a crazy American!" I liked her.

No matter how hard I worked at pronouncing Chinese names, I have a feeling I butchered them pretty badly. To me, Grace's driver became "Johnny"—about the closest I could come to saying his name. That second day, I found I could jest with Johnny. I learned that he was interested in Western ways, so Grace directed us to a Beijing hotel that serves pizza and other dishes associated with the West, and I had the pleasure of introducing Johnny to ice cream. I don't know when I've had such fun as I did that day, watching Johnny acquaint himself with America's favorite dessert. We bought plain vanilla, for Grace, Johnny, and myself. Johnny tentatively sampled it, his eyes sort of staring blankly—and then brightening as a smile relaxed his beautiful oval face. He took a larger swipe with his tongue and let out an "Mmmm." By then he was hooked. His spoon was never far from his mouth until he had consumed three orders smothered in gobs of chocolate syrup.

5

The Hair of a Great Ox

Before a CAAC plane whisked me away back home on Friday morning, the president of China Sports Service Company honored me with a formal banquet on Thursday night. The menu: Peking duck and all the trimmings, including succulent pork, "thousand-year-old" eggs, and several dishes I could not recognize. I would later grow used to the abundant multi-course meals these hospitable people serve their guests, but that night I couldn't believe all of that food was for us.

I was learning another thing about the Chinese—their way is to see that the guest has that "full feeling" three times a day. They certainly did their part!

In a dimly lit private dining room we gathered for the meal. Next to me sat the president of the China Sports Service Company, Mr. Yuan, and across from him was his vice-president, Mr. Chen. On my other side was Mr. Kong. By that time, I had grown comfortable around Mr. Kong, and he evidently felt the same way.

"From now on, you just call me Kevin," he said.

Mr. Yuan spoke only a few words in English. Of the dinner guests, some ten in all, only Grace and Kevin spoke English fluently. They helped me communicate with the others. Every effort was put forth to make me feel honored. As the meal progressed, we congratulated ourselves for having firmed up an agreement for The Great Friendship Run.

Waiters deferentially served us beverages and steaming dishes. Everyone was most kind in ignoring my clumsy manner with the chopsticks. Click, click went the chopsticks as each one helped himself or herself to ample portions of meat and vegetables, fish and noodles. Our conversation progressed easily; the more we ate, the warmer became the feeling of camaraderie in that room.

During the course of the dinner, Kevin said to me: "We know what kind of man you are, for we have watched you over the last three years. You have not given up." I was to learn that patience is a virtue the Chinese especially admire. They are accustomed to waiting, and waiting some more.

I felt at home with these people, like I was sitting down to dinner with some of the folks in Hart County, Kentucky. Commenting about the run, I said, "In elementary school, we had a time during the day that we called recess. This was when we took time out from our work and played awhile. We would throw a ball or chase each other. And when it was over, we would go back into the classroom. Somehow it all made good sense then. We were refreshed.

"This run will be very much like recess, when we can take time out from what we are doing and relax and play together. And learn to love each other. Then after the run, we'll all feel better. We'll understand each other better.

"I come to you as a child in the spirit of play, so that we take time for 'recess.' I don't know what our governments and our political leaders will make of what we do. I just come as one ordinary American who wants to make our world a little bit better than it was before I came here. All the world will benefit from this run, because we took time out from our work and played together."

"Gungshi! Gungshi!"

One of the officials wanted to know who were the prospective sponsors of The Great Friendship Run. I felt confident that some of our innovative corporations would want to get behind the run, for what it would do for them, if for no other reason. So I mentioned several by name. There was to be an insurance company, a shoe company, an auto manufacturer, and a major soft-drink producer, to mention a few.

The official responded, "For any of them to sponsor the run, it would be like giving the hair of a great ox." He was very animated.

He paused to swallow some tea while I wondered what was to follow.

"You tell the presidents of these companies that if they will give us that hair, we will give them in return a great ox. And they will be our personal guests too, when you come, and they will be friends of China forever."

What this man said touched me very deeply.

"You are different from the other Americans we meet," he said sometime later in the meal.

"Most Americans seem only interested in money. They are sometimes hard to deal with. But you appear not to be that way. Your ideals seem much higher. Do you think of yourself as different?"

"We all have to have money," I said, "and I'm like every other American in that way. I have to make a living for my family. Unfortunately, many of my fellow Americans are only interested in money.

"But other things are more important in my life. The things you cannot touch—reverence, respect, sincerity, honesty, truthfulness, kindness, patience, integrity. . . . You know, when I practice these, what I receive in return? Peace, kindness, joy, love, trust, gentleness, self-control, humility. . . ."

At that another man said, "You are a living example of the

Book of Proverbs." The blue-coated man surprised me, but he was totally serious. A young man, he was, with a beautiful smooth face and flashing eyes.

I had not expected such a comment from a man who I assumed was a Communist official. (Later I learned that few of them were members of the Communist party.) My jaw must have dropped when he said that. *Where am I?* I thought. I looked around me and felt such a warmth in that room—such peace, such love in the presence of my hosts.

I thanked the man.

"Proverbs are very important to me. I try to read a chapter from the Book of Proverbs every day." I did not know whether he was talking about Chinese proverbs, or what, but I went on. "Therein resides the wisdom of the ages."

"Gungshi! Gungshi!" they responded, raising their glasses in a toast. I had only been in China two days and did not know the exact translation of that word. But by the smiles on the faces of Mr. Yuan and the others, and the disappearance of the lump in my stomach that I had tried to ignore ever since our banquet had begun, I knew it must mean something like Cheers, Bravo, Right on! A toast from the heart.

"We will go forward with you," said Mr. Yuan.

The three days I had spent in Beijing, punctuated with two occasions for official discussions, had done nothing to erase my sense of awe. I felt I was truly out of my league now. And a little voice deep inside kept saying, *Who are you, a kid from Gobbler's Knob, Kentucky, that you should be in the capital of Communist China, talking with leaders in a branch of the government? Stan, you're a hayseed. These people have studied international diplomacy. You don't have any credentials.*

I was to return to China twice in 1984—in June to iron out details for The Great Friendship Run and in October to remain for fifty-eight days—fifty-three of which would comprise the 2,125-mile run from the Great Wall north of Beijing to Guangzhou, better known in the West as Canton.

6

"Barbecues"

The year 1984 commenced innocently enough. But I should have known to expect some trouble in the new year. After all, it was *Nineteen Eighty-Four*. Besides that, in the Chinese scheme of things, it was the Year of the Rat.

Rats are no strangers to anyone who grew up on the farm. They are a part of life. You do what you can to keep them at a distance, and under control. I've never known anyone who was fond of them—either two-legged ones or four-legged—nor are they the people's choice as a good-luck charm.

But if anyone had tried to warn me that the rat might be a bad omen for 1984, I'm sure I wouldn't have listened to him. I only allow myself two minutes of negative thinking a day, and that's when I brush my teeth; I just do not borrow trouble by worrying about what might happen. Nine times out of ten, it doesn't.

The road to China would include more cherished hours with my family. In January, our older daughter, Michelle, turned sixteen and Carol and I took the opportunity to make the occasion memorable. We arranged for a long white Cadillac limousine to pick up Michelle at school that day, with a formally dressed chauffeur, the whole bit. I know she was embarrassed by all the to-do, but she didn't seem to mind the ribbing she got from classmates the next day. She is very special.

The road to China would also lead through the Dominican Republic, in March, for I had been invited back there to do a benefit run for World Relief. Hugo Greiner, my coach and doctor, accompanied me there and assured me the run was "good training for China." On that run we chose a different route than I had taken in 1983, one that took us over rugged terrain. Due to the heat I developed a large blister on my right big toe and almost had to quit running. Then, to make things worse, I borrowed a sewing needle to puncture the blister and as a result sustained a severe infection, and I almost couldn't complete the 4-day, 160-mile hike.

"Stanny boy, this will get you ready for China," Hugo piped. "China will be many times tougher than this!"

I was finishing up the writing of *No Mountain Too High* and was planning the details of the China run with Tyler. We set a financial goal early in the year of $750,000 for everything—the China Sports Service Company fee, filming the run, plus editing and distribution. And we worked from the Memorandum of Understanding reached in Beijing to draft the final contract.

In June, I went to Jamaica and ran all the way around the island—four hundred miles—for the Caribbean Mission Board. More "training for China."

Later that month Tyler and I flew to Beijing to finalize the contract. With Kevin and Grace, we fixed the starting date—October 19—and the finishing date—December 14 (that would later be changed to December 10) and we agreed on the route.

China Sports Service initially wanted the $95,000 up front, by July, and it took intense negotiating to try to dissuade them. For three days, everywhere we went—to the Great Wall, the Ming Tombs, the Forbidden City—we talked contract with our hosts. I remember vividly the day they took us on a tour of the Forbidden City. In Tiananmen Square, where easily a million people can assemble, our negotiations were temporarily interrupted as Tyler and I stood in amazement, looking at what must be the world's longest bicycle rack. We counted eight parallel racks that continued for at least a mile; and the racks were full the day we viewed them—a powerful reminder of China's millions.

We sat once for six hours in Tyler's and my hotel room, talking out how the run would be directed and writing the terms for filming the run. Finally we were relieved to work out a payment schedule agreeable to all parties—three payments of $15,000 on August 15, September 1, and November 15; and two of $25,000 on December 1 and December 10. This did not include money for the Beijing Film Studio, which would be responsible for filming the entire run.

I could tell something was bothering Tyler on this trip. He was not himself. Was his quiet, humorless behavior due to the difficulties of the negotiations, I wondered. Or was it a combination of culture shock and jet lag? On the second night I learned that was partly it.

"I've felt empty and drained ever since we arrived in Shanghai," he told me. "The people have treated us okay, but the very air is oppressive; it pervades everything. And it's not just the pollution. My first impressions were negative—our being herded off the plane at Shanghai like so many cattle, military police everywhere, the masses of people living such regimented lives. It's gotten to me . . . So many people here without the joy, without life, without Christ. . . ."

There were tears in Tyler's voice. I remember how I had felt the same dampening of spirit on my first visit. To see all those faces and know that God knows each and every one staggers the mind and blows your emotional fuses. We vowed to try to be sensitive to these people as we moved among them. Praying about it relieved our spirits.

One surprise during the negotiations came from two persistent representatives from the Beijing Film Studio. China Sports has a television crew and we assumed that they would do the filming of our planned documentary. But the Beijing Studio got its foot in the door and sold themselves to us. We later realized that they had made exaggerated claims about their services. They had worked mostly on dramatic features and had done only one documentary. But we were in no position at that time to know that they were unfamiliar with the techniques of documentary work. So were we! And we took far too much for granted.

Tyler and I returned home confident and eager to round up the sponsors and make the final plans *final.* We didn't kid ourselves into thinking that raising $250,000 (the combined payment to the Chinese) would be easy, but we had no idea it would be so difficult.

At times, the needed sponsorship appeared within our grasp, yet somehow it kept eluding us. The last week of July, with the release of *No Mountain Too High,* I thought, *Surely this will open the door for investors.* In a way it did, but not as I had envisioned.

Earlier that year a businessman had warmed to my ideas for The Great Friendship Run and had talked seriously about investing $2.5 million. Along with eleven others he would underwrite our expenses for the run and the film and allow us to do things the way we wanted—first class. He wanted to form a syndicate. But there was one stipulation—I had to put my Christianity in neutral for three years of the five under contract, which was the extent of their planned involvement in promotion. I knew I couldn't agree to that.

At the Christian Booksellers Association Convention, in Anaheim, California, where my book went on sale, a leading publisher had offered me $50,000 to carry their product wherever I went. At the same time a soft-drink company had all but promised us a large sum. A Nashville medical equipment firm verbally committed $100,000, with a pledge to bring me a cashier's check on August 6. And a major Christian organization had indicated they would contribute very big—the chairman of the board had himself given a $1000 donation.

At the CBA convention, over a meal or autographing a copy of my book, I got to talk with people with the means to help make the China dream come true. But I felt as though I were slowly being pressed in a vise; time was running out for the August 15 deadline and about all the training I was doing was workouts on the Hydrafitness exercising equipment the owner of the company had given me. I was running several miles as time permitted—but that's not ultramarathon training.

As so often happens when we reach God's time in a matter, we are not at first aware of how He is putting things together. Even when we think we know how God is working, we end up being surprised. That's one of the most wonderful things about being a Christian. I'm learning now not to put God in a box.

On about the third day of the convention I met Anna Kendall, a bookstore owner and radio talk-show host in Dallas, Texas. Anna impressed me as competent and sincere, with a lot of class. But when she spoke of interviewing me on her program, I was skeptical. I figured that Dallas was one more place I would get barbecued—my expression for the frustrating, dismal end result of so many offers that had looked so promising at first.

Bob Lossa, the Dallas-area sales representative for Revell, the publisher of *No Mountain Too High,* had given Anna a copy of my book, and she read it on her flight home. Not knowing how to reach me once I was home, she called Directory Assistance; the next day I received her call at my house in Tucker.

"Stan," said a drawling, friendly voice, "When are you going to be in Dallas? I want to interview you for my radio audience."

She went on. "Your book moved me. I see your vision for running in China. And I want to help."

I was traveling through Dallas the next week to meet with Jerry Brentham, president of both the Texas Baptist Businessmen's Association and Hydrafitness Industries, so I arranged to see Anna also. Both meetings were divine appointments. Jerry joined in to help underwrite the run and Anna became an "on fire" general partner. At the time all she had hoped to do was put me in contact with some people who could provide funds. But her commitment was to be more lasting.

All this time I was buoyed by what would come of the interest the several companies had shown in investing in the film and the run. When Tuesday, August 6, dawned, I was eagerly expecting something to happen. But one by one, all of my rising suns fell victim to the clouds of doubt. The soft-drink firm and the Nashville medical company bowed out. So did the Christian group—that hurt me more deeply than all the others. And I never heard from the publisher. To me, it was Black Tuesday.

The pattern seemingly played out a certain scenario every time. A prospective sponsor would become enthused and invite me to show slides of my running and of scenes in China, and to talk with his board about opportunities for Chinese-American cooperation. Everyone would shake my hand and pat me on the back, and I would be promised half the world.

But then came the inevitable phone call: "Stan, I don't know how to tell you this, but quite frankly. . . ."

Or, as was often the case, no one called.

When one major shoe company had all but promised to underwrite the run and then their chairman would not tell me to my face why they were withdrawing their interest, I thought, *I've been to this barbecue before.* I *had* been to the barbecue before, and I was the one being barbecued!

A few of the companies we were approaching for aid had already committed funds to the 1984 Olympic Games, and could not help us. Also, about this time the runner Jim Fixx died, and corporate barons were understandably queasy about pouring money into a long-distance runner's event. What if I were to drop dead while attempting the Beijing-to-Guangzhou run?

But Anna wasn't giving up, and I flew back to Dallas a second time to meet her husband, Fred, and their friends, Francis and Catherine Galloway. They called Francis "Big Daddy" and I could see why. This sixty-nine-year-old retired businessman was tall, warm, and caring. He exuded love from every pore of his body. I told him that my dad was no longer alive and asked him if I could adopt him as my "Big Daddy" too.

"Why sure," he said, giving me a bear hug.

A board member of Christ for the Nations in Dallas, Francis had visited China three or four times, leading tour groups of Christian singers. He saw something of the possibilities of The Great Friendship Run and offered to help. What a boost these Texans gave me—and with their help we met the first two payments.

Weeks away from the start of the run, we began paring the dream to real-life proportions. Hoped-for commercial sponsors had not materialized, so we dropped the tour package and the new car we wanted to present to the China Sports Service Company, and the still photographer, and the trip for Carol to China for the start of the run. My friend Hugo stood in the wings and we finally had to scratch him as far as the beginning of the run was concerned—the money wasn't there. As October arrived, it was just me and Mickey Grant . . . and Jesus.

7

Getting the Cast Together

From the beginning, when The Great Friendship Run was just an ambitious, adventurous dream, I had the idea of capturing it on film. When I talked to Tyler about it, he agreed.

"Something of that magnitude, that important, should be filmed," he said. "A travelogue of China as you see it—that could be wonderful!" To our knowledge, a film of this type had never before been attempted.

That settled it. From then on, the run and the film were inseparable elements of what I hoped to do in China. But what did I know about making a film? Nothing. I figured the place to start was to find a film director. But I didn't know any. If I were to write out a description of the man I was looking for, how would it read? Mentally I listed the necessary qualifications:

1. Professional excellence and experience with document-
   aries.
2. A congenial personality; if not a friend, at least not an
   enemy.
3. Someone sympathetic to Christian values—ideally, a
   Christian.
4. Someone zany enough to desire what I desired—to make
   this dream a reality.

Those minimum requirements would have guided me in
the selection process. But, thankfully, I did not have to go
searching.

Miss Contact USA—that's my name for Anna Kendall—
took me to the Channel 39 studios in Dallas the second time I
met with her. "I want you to meet Roger Baerwolf, the vice-
president," she said.

While she and I were talking with Mr. Baerwolf, in walked
Mickey Grant, a blondish young man with rugged features,
wearing black rubber-sole shoes. I remember wondering why
he wore such ugly shoes! It turned out that he had recently
undergone foot surgery and could not wear regular shoes yet.

"Oh, Mickey, there's someone here I want you to meet,"
Anna burst in. "This is Stan Cottrell."

Mickey Grant worked for Channel 39 and managed a sub-
sidiary of KXTX-TV, Continental Productions. No lights
flashed in my head. I shook his hand as I have a thousand
others, and our conversation went on, now four-way. In time
Mickey learned that I was going to China and of the film we
planned.

"Do you have a director?" he asked.

Looking at him, I noticed for the first time how fair-skinned
he was. *He must stay out of the sun all the time,* I thought.

"No, I don't."

"I'm interested," he offered.

And that was the start of it. Roger and Anna filled me in on
the details of Mickey's experience right away—over a hundred documentary films, probably five hundred commercials.

"He's just come back from Egypt where he produced and

directed the live televising of a camel race around Cairo's pyramids," Roger said. One thing for certain about Mickey; he fit the wild and zany mold!

"China really interests me," Mickey butted in. "I lived in Taiwan for three years, working in films, and I can speak Mandarin—though it would be pretty rusty now. This China run sounds like an opportunity too good for me to pass up."

"Mickey's really understating his credentials," Roger explained. "He not only speaks Chinese, but for a project like this, you couldn't find anyone in the United States better and more competent."

When Mickey and I agreed to team up for the run I wondered how I could afford him. Seeing that Mickey could help me—and that's an understatement—Roger committed the station to pay Mickey's salary while he was in China.

Wow! I'm still amazed that Mickey, with all his expertise and his knowledge of Chinese, was available for the run. And he was an active Christian as well.

"Big Daddy," whose counsel I relied on, checked into Mickey's background. Being a businessman, he wanted to know something about the man we were charging with the responsibility for the film.

Afterward he told me: "Everyone I asked said, 'Mickey Grant! Mickey is one of the best men in the business.'"

"How do you want me to work with you?" Mickey asked. "What do you envision my responsibilities to be?"

"Listen," I said. "You're the expert on movies. The film is yours. Do it!"

"That's mind-boggling!"

From then on our American cast for the run was complete. As September passed into October, Mickey and I talked by phone and laid our plans. He would precede me to China to make everything ready so that we could begin shooting the film on starting day, October 19. I had my hands full raising—or trying to raise—the financing.

Each day I worked out on the leg machine. What a way to train for a two-thousand-mile run! I needed to be doing at least a hundred miles on the road each week, but instead I was flying here and there to speak and to represent our investment opportunity—and getting barbecued. But having come so far, I wasn't about to give up.

Mickey flew to Beijing on Friday, October 12, several days ahead of me, to meet with the people we would be dealing with from the Beijing Film Studio. At that point we had paid $30,000 to China Sports; now we needed $65,000 for both the film studio and China Sports and we didn't have a nickel of it.

The day before he was to fly to China, Mickey learned that Roger was leaving Channel 39, which raised questions about the station's commitment to keep Mickey on salary in China. I knew that I could not pay Mickey, if Channel 39 backed out; the run hung by a thin thread.

Still, Mickey proceeded until midnight Thursday to pack his bags. At 12:30 he dropped into bed exhausted. While he slept, we were engaged in crucial talks with potential investors. At 4:00 A.M. and again at 6:00, Anna called to tell Mickey that our meeting had not been successful. I felt like a zombie after that all-night session. My first instructions were for Mickey not to go. But by daybreak, my feeling was to send him on. Mickey himself felt that if he didn't catch the Friday morning flight, we might as well forget about a film because he would need four or five days to make minimal preparations.

With only $100 in his pocket and no contract for the film, and the promise that someone would meet him in Beijing, Mickey left on a Pan Am flight that morning. The toughest part for him was kissing Lois and their ten-month-old Christopher good-bye, but he had a gut feeling too that he should go. Only he wasn't sure if his gut was telling him that he had just missed breakfast and a good night's sleep and was now on his way to a fiasco, or what.

"Anyone I know," Mickey told me later, "especially those who love to claim how professional they are, would not have been on that plane that day. So, I must have a little bit of what you'd call 'runner's insanity' in me."

Mickey's arrival reassured the film studio and the officials of the China Sports Service Company. They now believed the run would materialize. But for Mickey, the arrival was, as he would say, mind-boggling. Being greeted at the airport by people who introduced themselves as the "producer" and the "director" of the documentary shocked Mickey.

"I had read the résumés of these people while in Dallas," he told me later, "but no one told me they would be producer and director. I knew that that was what you had sent me to do. The Chinese do not know how to make entertaining films for the American audience. How could they direct the film?" Mickey kept quiet about the confusion of duties and the finances and rode out the storms of the next several days until I arrived.

Tyler and the others questioned whether I should go to Beijing, since we did not have the money. But Mickey's being there left me no choice. It was unfair to Mickey to face the music—if it came to that. I had to go.

On the night before I left, Reid Hardin of the Baptist Home Mission Board in Atlanta, and his wife Phyllis gathered at our home along with another couple and Tyler. We prayed together and they laid hands on me, commissioning me a missionary to China for the run. At that time Reid read this passage from the Bible:

> Therefore, since we have so great a cloud of witnesses surrounding us, let us also lay aside every encumbrance, and the sin which so easily entangles us, and let us run with endurance the race that is set before us, fixing our eyes on Jesus, the author and perfecter of faith, who for the joy set before Him endured the cross, despising the shame, and has sat down at the right hand of the throne of God. For consider Him who

has endured such hostility by sinners against Himself,
so that you may not grow weary and lose heart.

Hebrews 12:1–3 NAS

This added a whole new dimension. In our den at home—
where only three and a half years earlier I had told Carol that I
wanted a divorce, and where the thought of anything Christian would have been a joke to me—we were praying and
thinking missions!

I recalled something that night that I had repressed for
years. An aunt had told me that Dad had actually wanted me
to be a minister. When I questioned Mom about this, she had
confirmed it. That night, recalling this dream of my dad's in
the midst of that warm, supportive circle of praying friends,
the run became for me more than an endeavor for friendship.
It was now a mission, a manifest destiny. My prayer that night
became, ". . . by this run may God have a victory," just as
David boasted after slaying Goliath, ". . . by my hand God has
had the victory."

A couple of months earlier a man had waited to see me following an interview at a radio station. He said he had a premonition that I was to pick up and somehow continue the work
of the Olympic runner and China missionary Eric Liddell of
Scotland. I had read of Eric and was profoundly challenged by
his life after seeing the film *Chariots of Fire*. To be compared
with him seemed absurd, for he had followed Christ with
such singular vision, putting Him before all earthly desires. I
felt as John must have felt, who, when compared with Jesus,
said he was not worthy to unlatch His sandals. In the days
ahead, when I would grow weary and fall prey to doubts, I
would draw strength from Eric's example, and from the
greater example of Jesus, "the author and perfecter of faith,"
and thereby discover renewed energy to keep running.

8

The Making of a Dream

Flying across the Pacific I had hours to prepare myself mentally for the unknowns I would encounter once I disembarked in Beijing. It was too late now to run the miles I needed to run to bring myself to the peak of conditioning for this ultramarathon. I would literally have to run myself into condition. *Believe,* I told myself. *Believe!*

While the odds against me appeared horrendous, I put my mind on the breakthroughs, the successes we had experienced thus far. Also, I tried to bring the run down to size and not get carried away with the excitement of this grand dream that seemed now to be almost within my grasp. Realizing one's goals means doing the next thing, and now the *next thing* was the run itself.

Watching the blue Pacific far below, I thought back to the day while, on a training run, I stopped by the road to scratch out in the dirt a formula that had crystallized in my mind. Since that day I've built a simple motivational message around that "Formula for Success" and given it countless times in motivational talks at sales meetings. It goes like this:

$$2V + \frac{E^n}{\triangle} = R$$

Visualize and Vocalize plus Energize (to the nth power) = Realize

The circle is a part of it because it represents the individual's life. So many people are going in circles, round and round. They have no definite goals other than quitting time or the next paycheck. To me, going in a circle means living a normal, ordered life. The planets travel in a circular path around the sun, and the year follows a plan: spring, summer, fall, and winter—and back to spring.

In my mind, a single circle represents one goal or dream or vision. I place the whole formula inside that circle because it is my success formula for achieving that objective.

The first V represents Visualize. Dreams and imagination are among the great gifts God gives man. The Bible says, "Without a vision the people perish . . ." (Proverbs 29:18).

George Bernard Shaw said, "You see things as they are and ask 'Why?' But I dream things that never were, and ask 'Why not?' "

Everything we do, whatever we become in life, starts with a vision. Now, to some people, vision is a scary word. And dreaming is placed in the same category as daydreaming. But they aren't the same at all. I've always had dreams: getting off the farm in Kentucky, earning a college degree, getting married, buying a certain suit of clothes or car, living in a certain kind of home, and, yes, running in China. Everything I have ever done began with this simple step.

Part of the Visualization step is seeing yourself doing what you want to do. And to do that, you must be realistic with yourself.

My friend Steve Bartkowski, of the Atlanta Falcons, is to me one of the all-time greats. I've watched him drop back and throw the football fifty, sixty, even seventy yards.

For a brief second I might imagine that Stan Cottrell is throwing the ball. But reality brings me back to the present. Could I do what Steve is doing? I look at my five feet eight inch 137-pound frame and I laugh. On the inside I feel like six feet eight inches and 230 pounds, but realistically I have a physical limitation. I had better not let my imagination run wild or I'll find myself reporting to pro football camp . . . and then to the hospital.

Take my decision that running the Great Wall was something I should look into. For most people, that would be an unrealistic goal. But I had been running long distances for several years. If I had known that I would have had to wait four years before Realizing my dream, I might not have tried it. But I've learned that every vision will be made real if we have patience. The majority of people throw in the towel too early; they don't have what I call "frustration tolerance." I see people making preliminary attempts at a variety of things one week, and the next I find they've called in the dogs and poured a bucket of water over the fire! The fox chase is over before it even started.

The second V represents Vocalize.

So many people keep to themselves and never talk about their dreams. What a pity. They live in their little private worlds, afraid to share the dreams of their heart for fear of ridicule.

I love to talk about my visions—with selected people. "Without wise counsel, your plans will be frustrated," says a Proverb. I take that to heart. All of us need an inner circle of friends, a psychological support group whom we trust to give us candid, frank thoughts on our plans.

The first person with whom I share my visions is my wife. After the children are in bed, we may sit around the kitchen table and that's a time to share our dreams. If Carol goes into a state of shock when I tell her what I'm thinking, I know I had better rethink my dream.

Part of the Vocalizing process is writing down the pros and the cons and talking about it with a trusted friend. I do this with my friend and attorney, Tyler. He listens and asks questions. (Sometimes he says, "Stan, that's just plain dumb!") Once in a while he's wrong!

The more I Vocalize, the more a reality my dream becomes. For myself, I try to bring my vision to God also. "Lord, I want to fit into Your picture rather than trying to fit You into my picture." I believe He has a plan, and I only want the best of the best of what He has in store for my life.

"Is China a part of Your plan for me, Lord?" I ask. In the four years prior to the run, I asked that question of God a lot of times.

The third step is Energize. This is where the rubber meets the road; it separates the men from the boys, the champs from the chumps. It is the work phase. I call this also the "wonder" stage, because while you are working to make it happen, you wonder if it ever will.

Lots of folks dream, and some talk about their dreams. But few take this critical step—to Energize. It requires a leap into the unknown; it involves effort. No longer a sideline spectator, you are in the arena as well as the pressure cooker. Your goal is far away. You have gone through the *wonder* phase so long and now it's time to put some *thunder* into the design and fashion of your heart.

Actually, this stage may begin as quietly as picking up the telephone and making a call. Or writing a letter. Or filling out a résumé. Or driving to see somebody. Fear keeps 90 percent of the dreamers from ever Energizing.

When I was a boy, Momma used to tell me stories of the sillies. In one story, Josh heard his playmate Elma Jean crying in the smokehouse. She was crying her heart out. Josh went in to see what was the matter and Elma Jean said, "Oh, Lordie, I'm just so sad."

"Why?" Josh asked.

"Do you see that big hammer on the shelf?" she asked.

"Yeah."

"Well, I was just thinking, what if James and I got married and we had a baby, and that baby grew up to be ten or twelve and was out here playing one day. And what if that hammer fell off the shelf and hit him on the head and killed him? I was thinking how sad I'd be."

Like Elma Jean, many people get bogged down worrying over what may never happen, and so they refuse to Energize. My run across the United States all began with a phone call. And I probably called 700 prospects to find a sponsor for that run. But it never would have happened if I had worried about "what if?".

The Energize phase requires tremendous commitment. That's why I write the formula—Energize to the nth power. To Realize requires a lot of work, but we all have access to an unlimited source of strength and power to accomplish extraordinary things.

Essential to the Energize stage is enthusiasm. I have been to sales meetings where the speakers have done everything they could to build enthusiasm—because you can't sell without it. But after a couple of days, the "adrenaline" I absorbed from that highly charged atmosphere was gone. I was on my own. I had to supply my own enthusiasm.

I've studied the word *enthusiasm* some, and I have found it means "God within." To realize that God is within me, and that I'm created in His image, is to begin to fan the flames. From there it's not difficult for me to expect things to happen. To Energize is to walk with expectancy, to speak with expectancy, to plan with expectancy. Enthusiasm and expectancy go hand in hand. John Wesley said, "Every day I set myself on fire with enthusiasm and people come from far and near just to watch me burn."

We have on our shoulders the greatest computer ever created. IBM could never begin to match it. Our brain has an infinite capability for Energizing—yet we constantly short-change ourselves by failing to use it. We need to elevate our cerebral machinery.

Under the $2V + E^n$ I draw a line and put the triangle, the Greek letter *delta*. I learned in chemistry that this means to apply heat, and heat brings about change. To heat water means to change its constituency.

The word *delta* is suggestive also. While flying on Delta Airlines, I studied their trademark, the triangle; it is broken into three parts—red, white, and blue. A flame is comprised of three parts. We know that the red represents the least hot part. Some people are like that. They are not as hot as they could be. They are burning, but not blazing. In spectrophotometry we can tell by the color of the flame the impurities that are being burned off. I like to think when we are on fire impurities such as doubt, dejection, worry, self-pity, anger, animosity, and greed are burned off. And they are replaced by certitude, faith, hope, self-confidence, joy, happiness, unselfishness, kindness.

I see in the delta triangle also the Trinity—God the Father, God the Son, and God the Spirit—working in me to Energize toward my goal. In Ecclesiastes 4:12 we read, "A cord of three strands is not quickly torn apart" (NAS). My faith allows me to visualize the indwelling, Energizing forces of the Trinity, making me strong to run toward my goals and objectives.

The triangle also represents the strength that comes through human ties with those closest to me—my wife and a few friends. I have learned that a dream that is shared by a closely knit team is hard to defeat. As one shares his wisdom and insight, he receives correction and encouragement from the others.

I draw a straight line under Energize; it represents a platform for me to stand on. Before 1981, without God, I didn't have a leg to stand on. But with Christ I have a source of strength that is more than mere words. That power Paul stressed when he said, "I can do all things through Christ which strengtheneth me" (Philippians 4:13). God, together with individuals, gives me a platform from which to reach toward Realization, the last phase of the formula.

I draw the symbol for infinity after the R, because we never cease to Visualize and create new objectives. When we realize one goal, we draw another circle, and another, and the process goes on and on.

As I stared out the window of the CAAC jet, energizing for all I was worth, the blue-green sea below spoke peace to my fragile emotions. Tomorrow I would need all the positive thoughts I could garner.

At the Beijing airport I looked forward with mixed emotions to meeting Grace and Kevin. We exchanged hugs and handshakes at the gate, but because I didn't have the payment with me, I was on guard against any negative message I might unintentionally send their way.

Once in the car for the ride to the hotel, Grace asked, "Why didn't you come with Mr. Grant?"

"Because of family problems," I replied. "Since I was going to be away for two months, there were some things I had to take care of."

"Where's your Dr. Greiner?"

"He couldn't come with me, but he'll be arriving later." (I honestly thought that at the time.)

"What about Tyler?"

"It wasn't possible for him to come with me. He'll be here for the banquet though."

I figured she associated Tyler with the money we owed, and I fully expected her next question to concern the payment. But that was never asked.

"And what about the photographer?"

Grace meant the still photographer we had planned to have with us. "Family problems," I answered.

This arrival at the People's Republic was not exactly as I had dreamed. Here I was, checking into the Yanjing Hotel on a shoestring. The official banquet in the Great Hall of the People would be Thursday night. The Great Friendship Run would begin the next morning—or would it?

In Mickey's hotel room on Tuesday I felt very frustrated. If things aren't going right, I can usually phone for help. But in

China you can sometimes wait twelve hours before you get your party on the phone. All I could do was wait and pray.

The stress Mickey had been through since arriving in China showed. For five days the Chinese had asked him where the money was and when would I arrive. On top of that, Mickey had been planning with them how they would shoot a very difficult film, using a large investment of money donated by Christians—a film that had great possibilities, but for which few preparations had been made. And he would be responsible for the film! With all of this on his mind, he had been unable to sleep.

Now as he talked, he paced back and forth, gesturing with his hands. He was visibly shaken. We didn't know what to expect. We feared for Grace's well-being, for she, with Kevin, had led the way in working out the agreement for the run. If it should fall through we weren't sure what might happen to her. She might lose her job. Could she even go to jail? And might two Americans be behind bars also? Is this the stuff of which international incidents are made? we wondered.

I did the only thing I knew to do.

"Is this 'No,' Lord? It can't be . . . I'm confused. I don't know where I'm being led right now . . . but I believe in You. And I praise You. You have told us, 'In everything give thanks.' I lift this run to You and I look to You. . . ."

I wanted to slip out of the hotel and go for a walk, to avoid any confrontation with Grace. But before Mickey and I could leave the room, in walked Grace, without her usual smile.

"I want to know what the situation is," she said, punching out her words deliberately. Working to control her emotions, she stood directly in front of me. "Do you have the money that was promised?"

"It'll be all right tomorrow," I ventured. "Sit down, Grace, and let's have some tea."

"When I ask you a question, why do you try to talk to me about something else?" she said, her voice almost shrill. "I have questions to ask you."

I stalled, not knowing what to say.

"If you do not have the money by tomorrow, the banquet will be called off. The run will be cancelled. There will be no reprieve. I want to know. Why isn't Tyler here?"

She knew that if he was not already en route, he could not arrive in time for the banquet.

"He'll wire the money tomorrow."

"That's not satisfactory," she insisted.

"Is that it, then, Grace?" Was there no compromise, no more time, I wondered.

She was trying very hard to hold back her anger. If we had to call off the run, I knew that she would lose face. For her it would be, not Grace, but Disgrace. All along I had determined that, should something happen to prevent the run, I didn't want Grace to be hurt.

"Grace . . . I do not have the money," I finally said. "That's why Tyler didn't come with me. He stayed behind and has been trying to raise the money."

With that, she turned and walked to the door.

"You wait here," she said, and left. She was as white as a sheet.

Mickey and I looked at each other. "I am really scared now," Mickey said.

I was not scared. I was worse than that. A million hopes and dreams seemed to have washed ashore and were going to dry and die in the sun if something wasn't done. But I knew that we weren't in a hopeless situation. Helpless, but not hopeless.

"Let's pray," I said to Mickey, grabbing his cold hand.

A number of Grace's associates had assembled in a room down the hall, evidently waiting for her to bring them news. After she joined them, their "discussion" commenced. Their voices rose in a rapid-fire cacophony of indistinguishable Mandarin, which Mickey and I could hear as we sat frozen in his room. For almost a half hour it went on without letup. *What will happen?* I wondered. *Will they force us to go home? Will they call the police? Or the American Embassy?*

In time, the volume dropped and the voices moderated.

After what seemed like an eternity, Grace reentered the room and walked determinedly to where I stood.

"We will start the run," she said. "We will trust you. But you must know this. If there is no money in ten days, we will stop the run."

There was no feeling, no expression in her voice. I think I managed to say, "Thank you, Grace," and breathed a deep sigh of relief.

She explained: "The banquet invitations have been sent. We really can't call it off now. Besides, we want to show our commitment to friendship and to The Great Friendship Run."

Those few words spoke volumes. They had to save face. But also, they were trusting me. I had been trusting the Chinese all along, while they seemed to make countless demands. Now, this go-ahead constituted a concrete expression of their trust.

Thirty minutes later, the telephone rang. Carol was on the line.

"Tyler has the money," she said. "He will be leaving in five hours to bring it." (It was 2:00 A.M. in Georgia, about 1:00 P.M. in Beijing.)

"Thank you, dear! Praise the Lord!"

Jerry Brentham of Texas and John Hedquist of Georgia, a former student of mine, had put up the $70,000 needed.

Grace sensed what was happening from the look on my face. When I told her the good news, she and Mickey and I let out a holler that must have echoed off the Great Wall. We hugged each other and laughed. We were ecstatic, like little children; we just danced in glee around the room, releasing all of the pent-up tenseness.

"Grace, you see, God does answer prayer!" I said.

"Yes! Yes!" she said.

When the excitement dissipated, I said to Mickey, "There's no doubt in my mind; this run will take place."

"Mind-boggling! Just mind-boggling!" was all Mickey could say.

That night, as proof of their commitment to the run, the China Sports Service Company moved me into a nicer room. It was like relocating from a truck-stop bed and shower to a first-class hotel. My new room smelled of incense. It had twin beds, a small desk, and private bath, with deep red silky curtains on the window and bedspreads of the same red material.

Thursday morning I awoke in that room, thankful for the breakthrough the night before. Suddenly the phone rang. Anna Kendall's drawling voice asked how I was, and I told her, "There are smiles on everybody's faces now."

We had one more agreement to firm up and that concerned the part the Beijing Film Studio would play in filming the documentary of The Great Friendship Run. We would have a large film crew, numbering twenty-two persons at times; two Arriflex BL cameras and two Nagra tape machines would be at our disposal, plus vehicles.

A Mr. Du of the studio staff came to my room that afternoon to finalize the contract. He was one of those who had startled Mickey upon his arrival in China by announcing himself as the director of the film of The Great Friendship Run.

Mr. Du was probably ten years Mickey's senior and he had represented himself as an experienced movie director. In truth, he was little more than a camera operator and had been appointed by the studio. As we were to learn the hard way, he had been handpicked for a task far beyond his experience. Furthermore, he did not understand English and spoke Mandarin with such a strong Shanghai accent that Mickey had difficulty understanding him. So we were badly limited until Grace joined us.

Being guests, and having just been given a vote of trust by China Sports, Mickey and I didn't feel we had grounds for rejecting out of hand the contract now presented by Grace and Mr. Du. So we waded in. With Grace's aid we began to learn the contents of the "contract" Du had brought with him.

Imagine our surprise when we read, among other things, that it called for me to supply the Chinese with seven new American cars! I had originally hoped to persuade an American auto manufacturer to provide a road vehicle and ultimately present it as a gift to China Sports; but I had not succeeded. When I asked Du about the seven cars, he assured me that it was not to be taken seriously; it was written in only to help him requisition the seven drivers needed for the vehicles the film studio would provide. I say "needed." As it turned out, almost half the road crew were drivers!

This contract was very ambiguous; even Grace did not seem to understand who was to do what. Mr. Du was insistent about one thing—getting credit for the film. Yet that issue was not even negotiable; Mickey would have to call the shots, for only he knew the Western audience, only he had the experience, and only he had been selected for that job.

We went around and around on this issue and finally agreed that Mr. Du would be listed as executive producer, Mickey as director. Tyler would soon arrive to straighten out the details, I reasoned. And besides, Grace and Du agreed verbally to the essential point—Mickey was to direct the filming—so we worked out the terms of the agreement. Trying to liven up the atmosphere, and at the same time give Du a vote of confidence, I said to Grace, "Mr. Du will be Head Daddy Rabbit!" But that backwoods expression didn't translate.

When the "negotiations" were all over, Mickey was optimistic. He would need to be.

9

A Night to Remember

"Our government doesn't care one bit."

Mickey put the telephone receiver down in disbelief.

"I call up the embassy and some woman says, 'Why are you bothering us about some run!' And then she hangs up on me! It's mind-boggling!" That was almost always Mickey's favorite expression.

How I wished General Loeffke were still at the Beijing embassy. He would have made sure that at least some of my fellow Americans would be guests at the banquet. Then an idea struck me. There must be someone at the embassy who knew something about running. I phoned the embassy once more.

"Hello. Is there anyone there who is a runner?"

A few moments later a very official-sounding voice filled my ear. "This is Gunnery Sergeant Laprade. To whom do you want to speak?"

"Sergeant Laprade, I may want to speak to you," I replied. "Are you a runner by any chance?"

"Yes, sir, I am . . . Why? Who is this?"

Finally I felt I was making headway. I explained to the sergeant who I was and that I wanted to invite the ambassador and his staff to a banquet at the Great Hall of the People that night, but couldn't get through to him. "Shag," as he called himself, said he would see what he could do.

The rest of the afternoon, Mickey and I contacted every television network with offices in Beijing, *Time* magazine, the Associated Press, Xinhua News, and several other news agencies, making sure they knew about the banquet and the run.

Then I heard a knock at my door. It was Shag, coming to meet me and to see if I was up to snuff. Before he left I learned that Shag did indeed know something about running. He had participated in several marathons and shorter runs; I felt that he understood my situation from the start. As he departed he said that he would pick Mickey and me up at 6:30 and take us to the Great Hall.

Foreseeing the contact I would have with the press as the run received attention, Mickey cautioned me against discussing politics with reporters. And that afternoon, the *Time* magazine Beijing correspondent, David Aikman, confirmed that bit of wisdom. He arrived at the hotel to interview me, and promised to follow through and see me when the run was completed, in Guangzhou, and I had the feeling he wanted me to succeed.

"In your dealings with members of the press," he said, "talk about your running, about the people you meet, not about politics." That bit of advice was worth a lot to me.

At 6:30 Mickey and I boarded a van filled with young men in three-piece suits with close haircuts—disciplined and mannerly fellows who would make our country proud. Shag said, "I didn't know how many you wanted, but I rounded up a van full."

On the way, one young man commented, "The folks back home will never believe this." I knew exactly what he meant.

The Great Hall stands imposingly on the Avenue of Eternal Peace in the vast Tiananmen Square, on the western side of the Monument to the Heroes of the Revolution. Our driver approached steel gates and showed the appropriate pass to gain entrance, past the military police who stood guard with automatic guns at the ready. A few feet away we disembarked and followed guards past two more security checks until we reached the elevator where Grace was waiting.

Upstairs we followed our noses as well as our proud hostess into an expansive, high-ceilinged, rather plain banquet hall, now stirring with formally dressed dignitaries awash in the light created not only by large chandeliers, but also by the Beijing Film Studio's lights. I felt a surge of pride for our country as I walked in flanked by a few—the proud—the Marines.

Seven huge round tables capable of seating at least twenty people each filled the near end of the room. Woodenly, Mickey and I followed Grace to our table, smiling at all of the strangers and accepting their warmth. I was glad to glance around the room and see that the marines had been seated at different tables in order to mingle with different officials present.

At our table was an official of the American embassy. On either side of me were the chairman of the China Athletic Association and the head of All-China Sports. Kevin was one seat away, and served as my interpreter. Other officials of the China Sports Service Company, some of whom I had met previously, were also at our table. All in all, about forty government dignitaries were at the banquet, I was told.

Some of the generous provisions that created the appetizing smells as we entered the room were now before us, on the largest Lazy Susan I've ever seen. One of these servers graced each table. On ours were heaps of noodles, vegetables, steaming rice, pork, chicken, ribs, and several kinds of fish, plus delicacies I could not make out (and wasn't particularly hankering to try at the moment). Without any fanfare, everyone started helping himself—very informal, with smiles all around.

It was seven o'clock and I knew we would have food before us for most of the next two hours. For once I was glad I had to attack all this delicious fare with chopsticks because I wasn't then very efficient with those implements.

From across the table Mickey eyed me as if to say, "Remember, you *do* have to run fifty kilometers tomorrow."

Barely ten minutes into the feast, a man at our table stood with a glass of *mao tai* in one hand and proposed a toast. I reached for my own glass of rice wine. Even one who doesn't drink, doesn't toast with water. And, there was no water, and I would not have been wise to drink it if there were. Someone had clued me in about the fiery *mao tai*. Ammonia couldn't open your nostrils any better than this strong drink. I call it "gasoline" because I'm sure a car could run on it.

With ample food and frequent toasts, the meal continued. The custom was for everyone to propose a toast, and so I took my turn, and really enjoyed it. After all, this was the hour of celebration and I thoroughly appreciated their lavish show of affection. From table to table we went, toasting and shaking hands, and I gesticulated as best I could to communicate my thanks and appreciation.

The further we went into the meal, the more frequent the words rang out: *"Gang bei!"* (bottoms up). Grace more than once came to my defense, knowing my predicament—that I wanted to enjoy the occasion totally and yet not overdo it. She would say, *"Bu gang bei"* (*no* bottoms up!).

Gifts of jade and a tablecloth were given to Mickey and me.

One official, I'm not sure of his position, toasted the run rather grandly. "This is the most important thing," he said, "that has happened between our two countries since the coming of President Nixon."

In my remarks I thanked them all for opening their country for the run.

"I look forward to running in your land. And I hope that the friendship between our two great nations will be made stronger by The Great Friendship Run. Thank you very much for your gifts tonight. Thank you for your love. *Zhong mei you hao wan cui*—Long live the United States–China friendship!"

"*Gang bei!*" they cheered. "*Zhong mei you hao wan cui! Gungshi! Gungshi!*"

The evening was all but over.

But never underestimate the Chinese sense of timing. After all this revelry, along came the head of the Beijing Film Studio with the contract that we had worked out earlier in the day. As the guests were leaving, he placed this agreement for the run in front of me and, smiling too much, handed me a pen. I felt as though a gun was to my head, loaded, with the hammer cocked! This was no time for discussion. I tried to glance over it. Beaming my pleasure outwardly, I signed it. The assembled onlookers broke into spontaneous applause. And I broke out in a cold sweat! My thoughts were, *Tyler is going to kick me around the block on this one!*

10

Some Think Me Odd

His name is Stanley Junior, his daddy's name was Stan
Some say he's an extraordinary, ordinary man
'Though college educated, he never did love school
But I'm a fan of Stan the man, the boy's a runnin'
fool*

A newspaper article in 1982, reporting on my proposed run in China, asked, "Do 800 million Chinese really give a damn?"

That question fairly accurately reflects many people's reaction to my dream. Not being able to comprehend it, they have ridiculed the idea. "So you run China. Big, hairy deal! What's that supposed to do? Improve the price of tea or beans?"

---

* "Stan Cottrell Runs for God" by Tom Taylor. Copyright 1985 — Thomas A. Bryan Taylor. Used by permission.

Others ventured their own creative explanation for the China run.

"Do you think this will make you famous?"

"You must be getting rich off this deal."

"Do you think women will hit on you because of China?"

Knowing how much my daddy influenced my life, one man said, "You're still trying to prove to your dad that you're not that wormy kid of thirty-three years ago."

Some were not even that kind: "You're two bricks short of a full load. Are you sure your elevator goes all the way up and down? You're a likable fellow, but this run in China has to be borderline sick in the head." An Atlanta radio announcer accused me of "exploiting running and the religious community."

Maybe there's some truth in those accusations. I really don't know. Perhaps more than I'm willing to admit, I am possessed of an insatiable drive because of my daddy. But as I took those first steps at the sound of the gun, within shouting distance of the Great Wall, I would have said, if anybody cared to listen, "I'm running this for the love of running. And if good can come as a result, then all to the better."

There's something about running. Virtually every long-distance run I've made, others have wanted to run with me. Running is contagious in some way. I discovered that the "bug" is alive and well in China. Running with me for the first kilometers on Day 1 was Mr. Chen, of China Sports. That in itself was the most unlikely scenario. Over the years during my numerous attempts to negotiate this run, Mr. Chen had been the "villain"—at least it had seemed that way. This very man who had sent telexes dashing my hopes in the past was now saying as we ran side by side down the mountain highway: "I'm glad to see this run finally starting. We will become friends before this run is over. For now, I wish you much success." A fine start for The Great Friendship Run.

The first several miles were downhill and easy. The air was brisk and traffic was light on the paved highway. The film crew wanted to stop for lunch after a few miles, but we were too far behind for that—at least, I was. Rather, I shifted into my regular routine—running fifteen minutes, walking five minutes, running fifteen, walking five.

When I did stop I asked for a drink and was given dingy-looking alkaline water which I couldn't drink.

"Sorry," said one of Grace's assistants. "Only kind you can get in China."

"You've gotta be kidding. I want a drink of good water."

"Maybe you like a beer," he answered.

"No, I don't want a beer. You can't run on beer."

Finally someone produced a Coke. Nothing tastes better at times, but you can't run on sweet cola either. Later I stopped and in near desperation chugalugged half a bottle of the mineral water, I was so thirsty. And still later, something carbonated, which I can only describe as a Chinese variety of 7-Up.

When I ran across Europe, I had recorded my experiences in a daily logbook. I wrote down the names of people I met and the places we passed through, significant facts about how my body was reacting, what we were having to eat, short prayers for God's help, thoughts that were filling my mind. But in China I decided to record my experiences and thoughts on audiocassettes. This would help me when it came time to write about it too. And so, that Friday afternoon I recorded some observations as I walked.

> My plans are to quit today at 4:30. I'm feeling tenderness right now in the groin area of my left leg. I think I'm going to end up with 43 or 44 kilometers for the day, and considering the time I got started, I think that's all right. . . . I've come through a lot of mountains already.
>
> I've turned south toward Beijing and now the land is totally flat. It's unbelievable here. The road is about six feet wide. For mile after mile there are sacks of corn along the edge of the road. . . . A lot of women are out here picking it up with shovels and putting it in the sacks. . . . I'm not going to take any chances, like trying to make 50 kilometers today. Hugo would be proud of me. . . . I thank God that I'm here. It's just a miracle. . . . We don't have any money. I don't know where

the next dollar is coming from. . . . The total cost of the run—$100,000 for 2,000 miles, figures at about $50 a mile. . . . It's hilarious the delineation they make between male and female here. They have one car for Kevin and another for Grace. . . . I don't know what is going to happen. If we can go all the way, and if the money will come. It troubles me. This morning I called Carol and she said there were a lot of prayers going up from Atlanta for me. That gives me great encouragement.

Up ahead, Mickey and the entire entourage had pulled over and I could see that Mickey was in a heated argument. I slowed my run to a shuffle, thinking I'd rest awhile. But suddenly my stomach was sending funny signals to my mouth and brain and I felt dizzy and weak. Frantically I looked for some place to sit down, but I never made it.

The next thing I knew, I was looking up into a ring of concerned faces. Blinking my eyes, I wondered who these people were. Then I saw Mickey, and focused on him; he looked really worried. I had blacked out and fallen down in the midst of a bunch of corn that was heaped on the roadside.

"Lift my feet, Mickey, lift my feet," I tried to say. "Lift my feet."

Mickey was worried about me, but he was even more concerned about the film crew.

"What are you doing?" he screamed at them.

They were doing nothing, except trying to help me.

"What do you think this film is all about? If he gets run over by a train, I want you to film it." He made his point, very definitely.

I had never passed out before from running. As I sat up and tried to get up, I could only think, *Stanny boy, you've got a long road ahead of you on this one!* As much as the jet lag, the cause of my passing out was probably dehydration, the mixed-up schedule, and no lunch. *We're going to have a meeting tonight and get this schedule straightened out,* I told myself.

I don't think I broke into a full run for the rest of the day. Part of the time Mickey walked at my side. I shuffled and walked until we reached the outskirts of Beijing, where we had agreed to stop for the day. We had covered 30 miles. Thirty miles down, 2,095 to go!

As would be the custom each day, I climbed into the *da puncha* for the ride to our night's lodging. With police sirens screaming, we passed all traffic on the roads back to Beijing.

At the Yanjing Hotel three pleasures awaited me. First, a delectable meal of many courses. I couldn't get over the amount of food they set before us. *At this rate you'll never have to worry about weight loss on this run,* I told myself. How wrong I would be!

They served us shrimp, chicken, rice (always rice), veggies, and fish, plenty of tea, with an apple for dessert. Fortune cookies must be an invention of the West, I concluded. I never saw one the whole time I was in China. I filled up on Coca-Cola and never worried a moment that the caffeine would keep me awake.

Second, Mickey and I had heard that we could get a massage for six yuan, or about two dollars apiece, so we lost no time in finding the masseur.

This was my first experience with acupressure. Working on the principle that *chee,* the body's "energy force," must be released throughout the entire body, the masseur kneads certain joints. Without oil of any kind, he would take my left hand and work his knuckle into the hollow between the base of my thumb and my forefinger. When he finished that hand, he would do the right hand. He worked down my body from my shoulders to my feet, massaging at the acupoints, pulling every bone out of my body it seemed. After an hour, I was wiped out.

The third pleasure that awaited me on Day 1 was bed! Somebody else would have to meet Tyler at the airport. My lights were out by 9:30. And that was to be a *late* bedtime compared to what lay ahead. We were often in bed by 8:00 during the run.

*   *   *

We had begun. Briefly before giving in to sleep, my body very stiff and sore, I recalled those special minutes I had actually been on the Great Wall that morning. The wire services evidently did their work because on Saturday, October 20, American newspapers carried a photo of me running on the Wall, wearing my stocking cap and white gloves, looking strong and confident.

The New York *Daily News* reported: "Runner hits real wall," explaining that "Distance runner Stan Cottrell of Tucker, Ga., sets off . . . on Great Friendship Run along Great Wall. . . . Stunt is being filmed for documentary."

The reporter, of course, was wrong about the Wall. I had started *from* the Wall, but not a yard of the run was actually done *on* it. His calling this a "stunt" irritated me, as though this were to be compared to swallowing goldfish or stuffing people into a telephone booth. To me this was a very special event, and to call it a stunt made light of all of the time and creative energy many people had put into it already.

Before I turned out the light, I noted on the recorder beside my bed:

> I mixed up some Phfrimmer [a mineral drink] and got some into me. I've got to get the liquids, hopefully tomorrow. One other note. Here they don't call people who are out of work unemployed; they call them "people waiting for a job." Right interesting! . . . Finally, I got the hang of handling chopsticks tonight. I've got about as much manual dexterity as a cow, but I was shoveling in the rice tonight. . . . Thank God for this first day. I miss my family. I knew it was going to be this way; it never gets any easier. . . . Especially, these last two months, I've never seen such support and understanding as Carol has given me. The road is certainly long. But I remember a few weeks ago the Lord spoke to my heart and said, "Stan, the road's not too long, if you don't forget Me."

All photos by Mickey Grant unless otherwise credited.

With prerun publicity photos, The Great Friendship Run was launched October 19, 1984 at the Great Wall, 30 miles north of Beijing (previous page). **(Wide World Photos)**

Along the roadway Stan stopped to visit with China's people, like the young dentist who pulled teeth for one yuan (left) and this duck herder (below).

Stan could protect himself from the rain and the cold, but the dust on China's dirt roads blinded the eyes and choked the breathing (above).

Mr. Wong, a driver for the Beijing Film Studio, made the going easier for Stan, greeting him with a towel and a "**Lao Peng-yo**" at nearly every kilometer of the run (right).

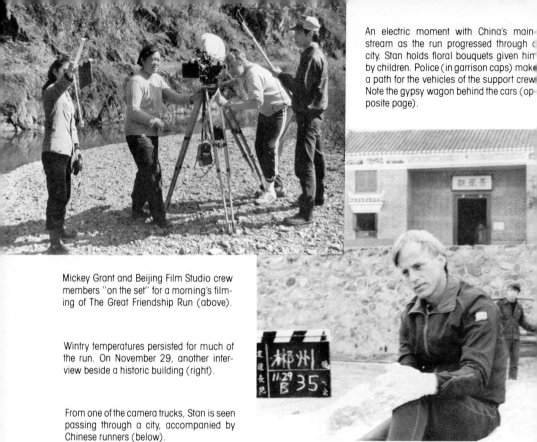

An electric moment with China's mainstream as the run progressed through a city. Stan holds floral bouquets given him by children. Police (in garrison caps) make a path for the vehicles of the support crew. Note the gypsy wagon behind the cars (opposite page).

Mickey Grant and Beijing Film Studio crew members "on the set" for a morning's filming of The Great Friendship Run (above).

Wintry temperatures persisted for much of the run. On November 29, another interview beside a historic building (right).

From one of the camera trucks, Stan is seen passing through a city, accompanied by Chinese runners (below).

The run wound its way south over mountain ranges, across clear-running brooks, and through terraced rice fields.

Stan takes a break
in the home of a peasant (right).

Welcomed by flag-waving, cheering greeters, Stan crosses the finish
line at Guangzhou, end of his 53-day, 2,125-mile run (above).
(Photo by Kong Qingwen.)

A joyful Stan wearing a floral necklace (left).

At the end of the day, the China Sports Service Company often arranged a fitting reward for run participants. Stan clowns, while CSSC coordinator Grace, Mr. Wong, and Mickey Grant prepare for the evening meal (right).

Following ceremonies at Guangzhou's White Swan Hotel, Stan displays the trophy presented to him by the China Sports Service Company for The Great Friendship Run (below).

11

"Things Can't Get Worse!"

"Stan, the higher-ups in the embassy really blew it on this one. This run is much bigger than they ever imagined."

My newfound marine buddy, Shag Laprade, was assessing the banquet in the Great Hall while we were readying ourselves at 6:00 A.M. for a full day of running. This Texan, whom I've come to regard as one of those special people God sends into your life just at the right time, was eager to run with me.

"Listen, that doesn't bother me," I told him. "Doing what I'm doing is plumb hard for people to understand."

Another *meigwo ren*—that's Chinese for American—was there in my room with me too. Tyler had arrived in the night, baggy eyed and beat and what was most important—packing money.

The plan for Day 2 called for me to run forty miles, and try to make up some of the distance we had fallen short the day before. But the simple matter of money threw a great big monkeywrench into the whole day's schedule.

Tyler had brought two cashier's checks for $25,000 each, and a $15,000 money order. This absolutely buffaloed the Chinese. They had expected *cash,* they said. At first they said that the Bank of China would not accept a check. *Here we go again,* I thought. *Another snafu.* In time, the bank gave the go-ahead and we were ready for the day's run—but it was eleven o'clock!

Interestingly, we sensed a change in Mr. Du's attitude from the moment the money was handed over. Du was in charge of the film crew and had agreed to work under Mickey's direction. Unwilling to admit that he couldn't understand English, however, he was always going in one direction while Mickey headed in another.

"It'll be a miracle if this run can be completed," Mickey lamented. "Du verbally agreed to the game plan I wrote out for the filming, but he told me it would not be proper in a socialist country to put that in writing!" What Du meant was that he did not want to acknowledge in writing that Mickey was telling him what to do.

I started the China run with a lot against me.

First of all, I wasn't in shape. I had been forced to spend every day developing a financial base, and that had knocked my training out of the window. Now, two days into the run, I could see that the Beijing Film Studio could be impossible to reason with at times. Also, the food was an unknown—I didn't know whether I could run for fifty days straight on a foreign diet. I've prided myself on being able to eat anything, but one evening early in the run, when they served up a whole soft-shelled turtle floating in a pot, I demurred.

"Eat . . . very good taste," they said. But I used an excuse they seemed to accept. "I can't run on turtle meat." The truth was, I was too much of a coward to try it.

In addition to being out of shape, confused about how to deal with the film studio, and somewhat put off by the diet I was being served, I was to encounter lodging along the way that made our cattle shed on the Kentucky farm look good. The lodging was quite unlike anything I had ever experienced, and it would get *very* interesting before we were done.

But the greatest difficulty of all boiled down to one simple thing—drinking water. And I do mean *boil down.*

I knew that I could not quench my thirst and restore my body liquids on the alkaline water they were supplying me. It tasted putrid even when cold. I had to have something else.

In America, we little consider how fortunate we are to be able to get fresh drinking water almost any time we want it. Until a long dry spell hits us, we use it to wash the dog or the car, to water our yards and gardens, to play in and swim in, to bathe in and clean with. We are so spoiled that a lot of us don't put a glass of water on the table to drink with our meal any longer. We drink other liquids instead. We can have water anytime, we think. Water is one of the "givens" of American life.

But not in China. The water supply seems to have been ruined. It's terribly polluted and even when boiled and filtered, it has a dingy appearance and a dull taste.

My new friend Shag had the solution to my water-pollution problem. Running with me the second day, he observed my obvious concern and offered me a five-gallon container he had in his room at the embassy.

"I'll bring it to you tomorrow when I come to run with you," he promised. "All you have to do is boil enough water at the end of each day, filter it, and pour it into the jug. By morning, your water supply will be cool and ready to drink. Not like what you're used to back home, maybe, but it'll do."

From the next day forward, Shag's water jug sat in a corner in the *da puncha*. I treated it as though it were a cloisonné urn full of the finest nectar. From its reserved spot it poured forth lifesaving substance—H_2O.

Another thing against me at the outset of the run was, simply, that I was running out of petroleum jelly. So sure was I that Hugo would be providing for such things out of his medicine bag, I had overlooked it when I packed. The feet can look as though they have been through a sausage grinder on a run like this. The experts have told me that for each time my heel strikes the ground while I'm running, a tremendous number of G forces (some six hundred pounds of pressure) clobber my knees, joints, and lower back. Ultimately, all of that pounding hurts my feet. If they could speak, they would cry, "Give me a break!"

While we were in Beijing I looked in vain for petroleum jelly in the Friendship Store, one of a chain of stores in China where the foreigner can often find what he needs. Again, Shag came to my rescue. A week into the run a package arrived via one of the film vehicles. In it were some ballpoint pens and a sixteen-ounce jar of Vaseline, compliments of Shag.

The sergeant thought nothing of these little favors. He hardly knew me, but he was almost ready to give me his right arm. It didn't hurt that I had served in the Marine Corps. Before he left to return to Beijing and his post he wrote in an autograph book I carried: "Best of luck to a crazy marine. Once a marine, always a marine. The Wall is quite a challenge. Go at it like a true marine. Gung ho."

I put in a call to Carol because it looked as though Hugo would not be coming, and asked her to send me Band-Aids, antibiotics, Pepto-Bismol, aspirin, vitamin C, and a few other items. I hoped that if she sent them air freight I might receive them early in the run.

I had made up my mind that I was not going to get involved with the disputes the film crew seemed to thrive on. I told them, "While you're having your daily argument, I'm going to go ahead and run."

The running battle with Mr. Du continued. "He cannot relate to us as the client for this film," Mickey told me. "He says he does not have to answer to us."

Grace had lodged us for the last time in the Yanjing Hotel,

so we had a two-hour drive on the morning of Day 3 to reach the point where I would resume the run. We learned that in that two hours we traveled 65 kilometers, approximately 37 miles (one kilometer is approximately five-eighths of a mile). The usual top speed on a highway in China (while we were there) is thirty miles per hour.

That morning, Tyler, Mickey, Shag, and I relaxed in the van, and once we reached the starting point, I began the day's run. It was 8:30 A.M., a big improvement.

I remember being very stiff that day as we set out. It's always tough at the beginning of a run, and this was the toughest because I had to run myself back into condition. You don't dare think about how far you have to go in the earliest stages—that would be asking for instant discouragement.

In some ways, the last part of a long, over-the-road run like this can be tougher than the start, because though you are in shape, your body is also extremely fatigued. Then the things that are happening around you—the sights and smells that you've gotten accustomed to—don't help pull you along nearly as much as the anticipation of finishing.

That Sunday, Shag and I ran together for almost five hours, running and walking, running and walking, until lunch break at 1:15.

Ten miles into the run, on the outskirts of Beijing, we came to a sign posted on the shoulder of the three-lane paved road: "Forbidden Zone," it announced in Chinese, English, and Russian. NO FOREIGNERS PERMITTED BEYOND THIS POINT.

China Sports had issued Mickey and me passes through the zone, and Shag was tickled to be along. Yet, there was little change in what we were to see that day. The terrain was flat. A railroad continued alongside the highway some fifty yards to our right as we headed in a generally southerly direction. Every so often, coal-driven steam locomotives passed, pulling their loads of freight and produce. On either side of the road were fields of corn, cabbage, cotton, and hay. The trunks of small trees along the highway were daubed with whitewash from the ground up to about the three-foot mark, reminding me of my boyhood days in Kentucky where this method of protection from insect infestation was common.

From the way the people glued their eyes on us, we must have been a curiosity. We were told that masses of these people never see a foreigner. Mickey took a start that night when a villager asked him in Chinese if he were a Russian!

Lunch that day turned out to be almost as grand as dinner the night before. But much of it I couldn't stomach, such as , octopus, squid, and dishes I couldn't identify. I was going to be running more in the afternoon, so I ate lightly. In an hour and a half, I was back on the road, this time without Shag; in another day or two Tyler would be leaving. On this road to Guangzhou, I would soon be all alone.

The lunch break gave me a new surge of energy. In fact, that day, I experienced a "natural high" for the first time since beginning the run. Physicians explain this euphoric sensation by suggesting that the pituitary gland secretes "morphinelike substances" called endorphins into the body; endorphins have the effect of overriding the pain being experienced and enhancing the pleasure. That afternoon I was "feeling my oats"; I leapt on the hood of one of the film studio's vehicles and pressed my face against the windshield, my nose mashed flat, smiling broadly. At first, they were startled, and then they laughed. They were beginning to loosen up.

I genuinely enjoyed meeting people along the road, waving at the soldiers and hugging the children, and saying, "*Ni hau,*" to everyone. Once, Tyler and I stopped to help a farmer empty the corn in her sack and thresh grain with a wooden fork. The people were shy, even afraid of shaking my hand. But when one brave soul would extend a hand, others would join in.

Shaking the hands of the farmers, both women and men, and feeling the toughened flesh reminded me of my own days on the farm. These simple people, but for their facial features, could have passed for the farm workers I saw every day as a boy in Hart County.

I naturally wanted to know where I was going to spend the

night, now that we had left Beijing behind. But Grace would only say, "A place has been prepared for you." I had to leave it at that.

Our lodging proved to be a cement factory, where a few rooms were maintained as quarters. That night I slept—or tried to, at least—on a board bed. My "mattress" was a pad about a half-inch thick. And for my head, I had a rice pillow. This is a small bag, approximately sixteen inches by nine inches, filled with rice and silkworm waste. It felt more like a sack of rocks than it did a pillow. In my accommodations, I awoke every hour or so, startled by the whining whistle of steam-engine locomotives. The building must have been twenty feet from the railroad tracks.

Our "bath" in these new digs consisted of two buckets of water. But at least things couldn't get worse, or so we thought. But little did we know.

The small, cold room smelled of mildew. But that was nothing compared with the indoor outhouse. I called these places "squatters" because, well, that's what you did. I dutifully went to one of them, but the stench almost knocked my head loose. I couldn't endure that and decided then and there to revert to my early childhood training in Kentucky and go out into the woods. For me, that was no problem. What was a problem, I was to find out, was gaining the privacy required. It seemed that I never felt the urge until we got near towns or to the places along the road where people were lined up to see us. And if I did manage to escape to a clump of bushes away from the crowd, the police were always near, keeping a watchful sentry.

At the end of the day, before going to dinner in the factory dining hall, I asked Tyler and Mickey to join me along the roadside. I wanted to thank the Lord and acknowledge Him, not in any showy fashion, but as naturally as I could. Grace and the members of the film crew were standing by and we invited them to join us.

"This is something we do that is important to us," I said, "and you can join us if you'd like." They all stood around and

I bowed my head and thanked Jesus for the day, for strength, and for all the people there, for the Beijing Film Studio, the China Sports Service Company, and for Grace. And they accepted that.

For over three years I hadn't kept my faith hidden under a bushel and I wasn't going to change now, halfway around the world. Tyler had run with me some that day, wearing a small cross around his neck which was given him by John Hedquist to pass on to me. We wanted to do something in a visible way that would be effective without being offensive to our hosts. At times I wore a T-shirt with the words, "Fellowship of Christian Athletes," printed on the pocket, beneath a small cross.

The church in China is largely unregistered; we never knew when we were in the presence of another Christian. But we wanted those we met or even those who only saw us on the road, to be encouraged. After all, we each serve the same Master.

12

My Old Kentucky Home

Monday, October 22, found me awake early. I blinked my eyes and looked twice around my bare room because I had wakened out of a vivid dream. I was talking with my daddy back on the family farm in Kentucky and it was so real I would have sworn that I smelled new-mown hay. *Why am I dreaming about Kentucky and the farm?* I wondered. *And why do thoughts of earlier days bring on such a wave of insecurity?*

Coming to China, I had felt secure and confident, but now I had to admit to a lot of anxiety. I had shrugged off the feeling, telling myself that it was natural to feel this way because I didn't know what lay ahead. Too, I was cut off from my family. It would be very hard for Carol to contact me in the event of an emergency. I would have ample opportunity to learn how hard it is in China to reach out and touch someone. . . .

Turning these thoughts over in my mind, I wondered at the lasting effect of my upbringing. I guess it really wasn't so strange that I would feel these painful emotions of insecurity when thinking of my old Kentucky home.

My brother and four sisters and I grew up on a farm near Munfordville. Being the oldest, I recall the earliest years when our house was little more than a shack. Momma carried water in two five-gallon buckets from the pond each day to heat for washing and bathing. Winters, when we were small, we bathed before the fire every Saturday night. In the warmer weather, Momma would take us down to the pond to wash.

Daddy ruled our Kentucky place as the undisputed head of our family; when he yelled, I knew I had better do as he said.

Daddy loved to hunt. In later years he proudly drove a Chevy pickup around Hart County with the words on the door, "I'm a fox hunter and a good sportsman."

Fox hunting means hound dogs, and Daddy always had at least ten tied up in our front yard. Only when I got older did I realize that other people didn't have to holler down the dogs for ten minutes before a civil conversation could be had with the newest visitor to the front gate.

Momma saw to it that each one of us young 'uns got a large share of affection, but we never got it from Daddy. He kept us in line with a word, and when that didn't do it, a whipping did.

Being the oldest, it was natural for me to take the brunt of Daddy's disciplining. In my early growing years a lot of that punishment was meted out because I simply wasn't growing the way my daddy thought I should. He stood six three and weighed at least 230 pounds. And he expected his son to measure up. But in high school my height topped off at five eight and a half.

Years before that, though, Daddy tried in his own crude way to eradicate whatever it was that was stunting my growth. No one knew dogs better than Daddy, and he regularly gave them a worming when they showed any tendency to remain runts. He attempted the same thing with me and my brother, Harold, and two of my sisters, Shirley and Mary. If one of us was irritable or peevish we always got a whippin' and a wormin'.

"You're plumb wormy," he would say, and there was no way to convince him otherwise.

"If you weren't so durn wormy, you could play basketball," he would tell me, with obvious disregard for my feelings. Sooner or later, despite the screaming and the tears, we all got our worming. But we didn't grow and put on weight like Daddy's hounds did.

I grew up believing that I disappointed Daddy in every way. Even though it makes no sense, somehow I felt that it was my fault for not getting taller. Daddy had been athletic and had excelled in basketball. He wanted a son to play basketball, and he talked about it often enough. Many times he would put his hand on my head and apologize to his fox-hunting buddies for my "puniness." I loved to run at a young age and I won my first prize for running when I was only twelve. But that meant about as much to my dad as a sidesaddle would to a hog.

He usually humiliated me about my height after he had been drinking too much. In my first eighteen years I saw Daddy drunk more than I want to try to remember. And when he drank, his deep-seated anger boiled up and he took out his hostility on us children—especially me, it seemed.

"I'm doing this to loosen up your hide to make you grow!" he would tell me.

One time when Daddy was feuding with the town constable, he got three sheets to the wind and drove into town with two shotguns in his pickup. In the middle of the street he stopped, fired several shots in the air, and hollered, "I'm looking for the constable." Wisely, the man never showed his face.

I hated being around Daddy when he was drinking. One time, my feet were painfully sore from what we called "dew poisoning." This happened because we children went barefoot all summer. Running across the fields, we would stub our toes and get cuts on the soles of our feet. The moisture from the grass would seep into the wounds, causing infection. Sometimes the swelling went up into our ankles.

Once when I had dew poisoning, Daddy wanted to see me dance.

"My feet hurt so bad. I can't," I cried.

"Dance, boy!"

"But, Daddy, I can't."

"At least jump up and down," he demanded.

I jumped up and down obediently. And as I did so I muttered, "Gosh durn, Oh, gosh durn!"

To Daddy, that was not innocent language. And he hated cursing in his children. He took a switch and whipped me so badly that I couldn't lie down on my back for a week.

"I'll teach you to cuss," he said.

His favorite expression for me, when he grew mad, was "You durned ee-dee-ott!"

"I'm not an idiot, Daddy," I would contest. "Please don't call me that."

"You're just a durned idiot!" He said what he wanted to.

For all his crudeness and raw bullying, I loved my father. And I think he loved me. Yet I never knew what it was to have his approval until late in Daddy's life. In 1979, my hometown of Munfordville, Kentucky, put on a "Stan Cottrell Day." Daddy and Momma sat with me in the place of honor, and I never will forget his remarks in a speech after dinner. For the occasion, Daddy was dressed in a new tan corduroy suit, and he told everybody: "This boy of mine has defeated the odds. I've watched him overcome all the obstacles and he did it. To be truthful, I didn't think he'd make it a lot of times. But he proved me wrong. He says now he's going to run clear across the entire United States. This time I'm listening to him." That night Daddy gave me one of his prize baskets that he had made himself and he said to me, "Son, hitch your wagon to a star."

Daddy bought another suit when he purchased the corduroy one, and he was dressed in the second one when he was fixed for burial two months later, in January 1980. He was in the hospital for a time and I remember going to visit him. We were both feeling awkward; I wasn't used to seeing Daddy lying in bed. I noticed that he had put a chain around his neck and that he was fingering a cross that hung at the end of the chain. He had bought the cross at an auction some years earlier, but I had never seen him wear it.

"A man who doesn't put God first in his life is really missing the boat, isn't he?" I said. Daddy looked straight at me and answered, "If a man doesn't put Christ first, he's a fool."

Just then the other patient who shared the room entered and Daddy introduced me to him. "Your dad's been telling me an awful lot about you," the man said. And Daddy added, "Yeah, and I'm awful proud of him, too."

Already, on several occasions while running in China, my thoughts had gone to my dad. I wondered how he would have handled some of the dilemmas I found myself in, dealing with the Chinese. He had been brilliant in his own right. He seemed to possess an innate ability to size up people. And if there was to be a battle of wits, Daddy would win it.

Daddy had felt incredibly secure with anyone he met. He was a wheeler-dealer in the best sense. He sold cars for a time and told people that he guaranteed they would get the car off the lot even if he had to push them! His cars were "cream puffs" . . . "knee-deep in rubber." The people loved his offbeat homespun humor.

He was rougher than a cob and tougher than a pine knot. With that toughness he instilled in me the drive to succeed in spite of the odds. Regardless of the early years, I came to love and respect Daddy. I remembered him, his face revealing the turmoil of some predicament facing him; but time after time he worked his way out of it.

I wanted now to plug into my dad's mind, to know his formula, to have his wisdom. But it's too late; I can't go back.

Before coming to China I had gone to the Cub Run Cemetery and lain across Daddy's grave. For over an hour I cried my eyes out, just talking to Daddy, not building him up larger in death than he was in life; I felt lost without him. *Why didn't I learn from him more? Why couldn't I have had the wisdom to tap my dad's mental reserves?* I cried.

As a young 'un, seeing everything in black and white, good or bad, I asked my mother, "Why do you stay married to Daddy? He's so mean and drinks so awful much."

She looked at me as though I had asked a question she had never thought of. "Honey," she replied, wrapping her arms around me, "I married your daddy for better or worse. I'm going to stick by what I promised."

"But he treats you so bad. . . ."

And she would hush me up. I never heard her criticize Daddy and she never allowed us children to either. I rarely saw any demonstration of affection between them, but it was there. We all grew up knowing that our parents loved each other.

Momma is a Christian. To this day every conversation I have with her ends with, "Don't forget the good Lord." She has always prayed and read her Bible. And she tried to teach us to live right. Through my youth and into manhood, those teachings stayed with me.

We honored our parents by quiet obedience. We learned not to criticize or question their decisions; to talk back would have been a disgrace. The code of the hills said that parents trained their children right; and being trained right meant you did what your daddy said without back talk or any sassing!

Momma prayed a lot. She used to tell me that she prayed for us every day. She also prayed daily for Daddy. And I will never forget the day God answered one of her prayers.

It was New Year's Day, 1961. Daddy walked into the living room and looked at us all for a minute. Then he took the big family Bible and laid his hand on it.

"With God as my witness, I'm never going to take another drink as long as I live," he said.

He kept his word. For the remaining nineteen years of his life, he never drank a drop of liquor. He didn't tell us why he had come to that decision; he kept it a secret. But one thing we knew; when Daddy made a promise, he kept his word.

"I prayed twenty long years for him to quit his drinking," Momma said. "The good Lord was a long time answering, but I knew He would be faithful in answering my prayers."

If Daddy had been in the room to hear me groan as I climbed out of bed that morning, he would have had little sympathy for me. Many time as a lad I heard him tell me— when I was facing some obstacle—"It's a bitter pill, but it's got to be taken. Get out of bed and get at it!"

As I set out on the road that day, I knew Momma would be praying for me. And just the thought of that encouraged me onward. That day I was on the road from 8:30 A.M. to 5:30 P.M. We traveled through farm country all day, seeing lots of cotton and cabbage fields. At the end of the day, Tyler and I were recalling some of the sights. We had been amazed to see all in one day:

A dead mule
A man hit by a train
Dirt and straw fence rows
Korean War MIG-19s screaming overhead
A red casket being towed down the road on a cart
Three sons being the mule as their father guided the plow
The multicolored hues of autumn in China's trees
Nine-year-old boys pulling humongous loads
Cotton drying on the housetops
Large mud-house kilns
Transmission towers
Sheepherders

13

"I Don't Want a Shot"

One thing I forgot to tell Grace about was "Even Flow of Energy Distribution." That became apparent on Day 5.

I had already run 69 kilometers by 5:00 P.M. that day and had left the road to retire for the night. But Grace approached and announced coolly: "You will run until we can see the sun no more."

"Absolutely not!" I told her. "I'm not running another step." I hollered for Tyler who came running from the van. Upon learning my fate, as just pronounced by the well-meaning Chinese director of this "forced march," Tyler backed me up. We were right on schedule. What was the need?

Grace and the other Chinese had been sort of amazed at this American who could run all day, and then do it again the next day. But instead of understanding when I would stop for a half-hour break, to take some liquid or just crash for a while, they kept cracking the whip. They didn't understand that in order to run a long distance the body has to think EFED—Even Flow of Energy Distribution. That is my formula for alternately running fifteen minutes, and walking five minutes, with a rest break every three hours or so. Tyler tried to explain it, but I'm not sure he succeeded. The sheer duration of this odyssey required, as Hugo would say, that I had to take it "nice 'n' easy."

The fifth day is remembered because on that evening Mickey, Tyler, and I took baths together. Riding in the gypsy wagon to our lodging that late afternoon, Mickey sighed: "I'm sure looking forward to getting a bath tonight." We all nodded our agreement. We had been on the road three days since the last bath in the Yanjing Hotel. Pollution poisoned the air in greater Beijing, and out in the countryside dust floated about as smoke from a grass fire. It was very dry. Running in powdery dirt stirred up by the bicycle traffic and boiled up by passing trucks, I was filthy. In the place where China Sports put us the first two nights, I had awakened each morning to hear people gagging and spitting, attempting to clear their throats. Some of that was from smoking, I knew, for the men seemed to smoke a great deal. But I imagine the larger reason for their coughing is that for years they have breathed this dust.

"I'm going to have lung disease and I've never worked in a coal mine," said Mickey.

What a relief to finally reach our destination that day and anticipate soaking in a hot tub. The three of us almost ran when the attendant called out: "Your baths are ready!"

But what a letdown. In a barren room we encountered three wash pans containing about three gallons of water each. So much for our fantasy of a hot bath!

On Day 6 my blue-eyed good buddy had to leave and fly home, and his leaving would touch off another minor tempest on the stormy sea of our relations with the Beijing Film Studio. That day, when I was struggling through a long stretch of road, Tyler sensed my fatigue and joined me for a spell.

"Hey, b-r-o-ther," he called. "Hey, bro!" Running along beside me, he got me to talking. Soon my doldrums had disappeared. His companionship meant so much to me. I never asked him to actually run with me—it was enough for him to run the legal and financial side of Friendship Sports— but I was glad to have company. One of the things we talked about that day was the big job now awaiting him, to raise $400,000 for the film by November 15, just twenty days away.

Before leaving, Tyler wrote out some directives to clarify the ground rules we had all agreed upon for the making of the film. But Mr. Du didn't much like the fact that Mickey would do the final edit of the film and wanted at least an equal share in that responsibility. Since the contract was first devised, it had become clear that Mickey had to have the final say because he was the only one who knew the Western audience for whom the film was being prepared. But Du chafed under that part of the agreement. He wanted more.

"But we're paying for the film," Tyler said, as though that should clinch the matter. "We are taking all the risks and we have to retain the rights."

In all of this it came out that Mr. Du thought Mickey a pain to work with. Mickey countered that the film crew seemed intent on making *another* film, not the film he wanted.

"They're shooting things such as temples and bridges and heaven only knows what else without asking me," he pleaded. The camera operators were quite competent, but in the early days of the run, Mickey pointed out, they made all the mistakes typical of students—leaving cables unplugged, using dusty equipment, failing to comprehend what our real purpose was.

When Grace and Mr. Du saw that Tyler was not going to back down, they called a meeting of the entire film crew, from which they emerged more conciliatory. The air had obviously needed clearing. I think that we and they realized that we had a long road ahead of us and for the good of the project we had better get along.

"We will cooperate with you," Mr. Du offered. And Mickey responded: "We'll work with you."

Grace asked Mickey to communicate more regularly with Mr. Du and she requested that we cooperate with a Mrs. Lu who, we were informed, handled the advance publicity, arrangements with the local political officials in the towns and cities and provinces we would enter, and the local newspaper interviews.

"I need to work more on my Chinese vocabulary—specially the terms related to film—so that I can converse with Mr. Du and the others," Mickey volunteered.

Before leaving, Tyler reminded me of the importance of my being discreet when speaking of my faith.

I had talked to some girls when I stopped for a rest the previous day, and had asked one of them, "Do you know about Jesus?"

"No, what is that?" she answered.

Tyler and I were concerned lest Mickey and I would offend someone and maybe even get someone in trouble.

The morning of Tyler's last day, Mickey came to breakfast with his little VHS camera, as he usually did—ready for action. He brought this amateur camera only to shoot a message for our wives. It happened that religious music was playing on the radio, and Mickey filmed Grace, Mr. Wong, and a few others listening with Tyler and me. I showed Mr. Wong, one of the drivers, how to make the sign of the cross, and afterward he told Mickey that he didn't like that. I was nervous—and probably needed Tyler's admonition.

The night before he left, Tyler asked me for the notebook of remembrances I was making. In it he added words that I would read and reread throughout the coming days.

> . . . always remember the reason you're here . . . to minister the gospel of Christ. Therefore our mission must be one of peace and friendship. This means we must control our anger and words. "Be slow to anger";

put away anger and should you become angry, "sin not."

"The angel of the Lord encamps round about them that fear him, and delivers them."

I urge you not to worry about your families. They are in God's hands. Your faithful prayers for them are not diluted by geographical separation. The authority of Jesus is not weakened by distance or physical separation.

Finally, you must exhort one another daily. My prayers will remain with you until I see you again. I love and cherish you with the love of the Lord.

At that early point in the run, Tyler wasn't the only one warning me. Mother Nature and Father Time were also talking. After Day 6 my knees were throbbing. A hot bath would have helped, but again it was the Super Special—bathing in a wash pan! I was grateful that Mr. Wong, who showed such constant devotion, wrapped my knees with warm cloths when I laid down.

I was also hearing another voice, that of my doctor friend, Hugo. "Stanny boy," I could hear him say, not mockingly, "every time you get out of shape it takes that much longer to get back in shape."

For someone who loves a soft bed, this run was the test! For most of the way I would go to bed on a pad about a half-inch thick that lay on a wooden frame, and rest my head on a rice pillow. By the time I had run three weeks in China, I had gotten used to these Spartan conditions, but in those first days I tossed and turned, my knees throbbing.

To complicate matters, I could not eat very much of what they set before us. Grace must have realized my plight because one day she made me a delicious bowl of noodles and broth for lunch—like none I've ever tasted—and served it to me in the gypsy wagon while dozens of faces pressed against the windows to watch this white American eat.

At dinner, Grace felt that she was honoring me by always setting my place at a table apart from the drivers, the police, and the camera crew. Usually she and Mr. Wong would sit with Mickey and me and provincial leaders; if Kevin or another official were there, they would sit with us also. And always they would place a screen partition between our table and those of the rest of our traveling group. I would often get up and remove the partition because I saw no need for it. But the next evening, the partition would be up again.

I'll never forget Grace's astonishment the first time she saw me bring my pills to the breakfast table. Hugo would have been proud, but Grace was bewildered.

"What is all that?" she asked.

"Those are my vitamins," I told her. "I'm beating the fool out of myself on the road, and this is what I need to put back into my body every day.

"I take three scoops of Nutri-sport, a mixture of minerals, and mix it in a glass of water.

"This is Aufbrau Concentrate B_6. I mix three scoops of it also and drink it.

"And I take a tablet of Vitamin E, a B100 capsule, and zinc, 50 milligrams. Plus some Herbalifeline with octocosonal, which I like very much. And cassandra, a vitamin-mineral supplement.

"I also take selenium, Vitamin A (10,000 international units), Vitamin D (400 international units), plus tablets of garlic and parsley. That's all.

"And then I do it all over again at night, except then I also mix up some Phfrimmer mineral drink in my water jug."

Now Grace thought I was crazy for sure.

At Xinle, Mickey and I enjoyed our first soaking hot bath. And other good things happened. We were feted with another banquet, and given presents. The Chinese are masterful with the massage, and we both received a magnificent rubdown that night. During the day, when I would take a break, Dr. Zhou, a local physician who traveled with us a few days, would give me a rubdown. I called him "Doctor Feelgood."

I had been looking for an opportunity to call home, and that night we were able to, with the aid of the old crank-type tele-

phone common in America back in the forties. Carol had encouraging news of press coverage on the run.

Also that evening, Mickey picked up a bit of an English-
language gospel broadcast on shortwave. I never realized how
wonderful it would be to hear English.

For all the vitamins I was ingesting, I was still losing
ground physically. The night of October 26 I awoke, my body
lathered in sweat. The weather had abruptly changed, end-
ing our unseasonable warm spell, and a cold rain beat upon
the window. In the morning I awoke with a temperature,
feeling weak and wobbly. I should have stayed in bed
that day. Mickey was the only one who knew I was running
a fever.

"How are you going to make fifty-seven kilometers today?"
he wondered. I didn't have an answer. Something was better
than nothing, I figured. Even if I had to saunter along, I
would be putting in a few miles, and every mile I could finish
was just one more I would not have to make up later.

I babied myself, walking most of the time that day. By 12:55
I had covered twenty-two kilometers, most of it with Mickey at
my side. We were hoping for a total of forty kilometers before
quitting time.

"This scares me," I confided to Mickey. "It could develop
into pneumonia. And then they would want to take me to one
of their hospitals." I figured I stood a better chance of getting
well *outside*.

Evidently I had not concealed my sickened state very well,
for that afternoon Mr. Chen, of China Sports, brought me
"some very famous Chinese medicine"—of herbs and spices.
Because I trusted him I thought, *Why not?* and took the medicine.

If I was scared all day, I had even more reason to be that
night. I had run—mostly walked—35 kilometers that day. I
staggered along, fighting for every step. I had to keep going,
but my legs were wobbly and I was burning up with fever. I
was scared.

I remember seeing the kilometer marker 218, and can

barely recall making it to the van and collapsing. Sports Service people helped me to my room, and meanwhile, Mickey and the film crew were recording all of this on film. It was high drama, I guess—the sort of stuff of which movies are made.

The next thing I knew, into my room came three people dressed in white coats, wearing white caps and masks. *What on earth has happened?* I thought. *Have I died and gone to heaven?* It was almost comical. They hovered over me, taking my temperature, listening to my heart, taking my pulse.

One said, "He needs a shot."

Well, there was no way I was going to let them do that. I know of horror stories about people getting shots, and all the cases I was familiar with had happened in safe, hygienic America! From my years selling pharmaceutical supplies I knew the importance of the medic's aseptic technique.

I resisted. "No way in the world are you going to give me a shot."

But there were more of them than there were of me. And I wasn't much stronger than a wet noodle.

"He must have a shot," they insisted, while one of them filled a syringe with some brown-colored liquid, probably a solution of herbs. They assured me that what they were giving me was reserved for dignitaries; they had had to go to the warehouse to obtain it. Small comfort!

I was screaming, "Mickey, no way! Don't let them give me a shot!" when suddenly I felt a thud and then a dull throb in my left arm. In thirty long seconds the contents of that syringe was in my bloodstream. "Chinese medicine very good. Will make you sweat!" said one of my masked attendants.

That night we were to eat supper in the home of a peasant family, so they bundled me up for the short walk there. I was so weak I could hardly walk—but the show must go on! Of course, I had looked forward to an opportunity to visit in the home of the common people, and Mickey and the film crew were prepared.

On our way to the house, we turned a corner and came

suddenly upon hundreds of people in the commune—men and women and children, mothers holding babies, a few teen-agers. All of them were staring at us.

The room where we were to eat was, I guess, about ten feet by fifteen, packed with our supper party, while dozens of curi-ous onlookers stared at us from the doorway and windows. I would have given anything to be able to read their thoughts. They served us an enormous amount of fish, vegetables, rice, and dumplings.

In China, nothing can draw the family together like the evening meal. The Chinese—perhaps more than any people, it seems to me—make a great ritual of food preparation and eating. A part of the explanation may be that the Chinese have always known hunger; to eat meant nothing less than to live. The normal Chinese greeting in the street is not "Hello" but "Have you eaten?" This does not constitute an invitation to dinner any more than our "How are you?" necessarily rep-resents an inquiry into another's health. It does, however, demonstrate how integral to one's well-being is a full stom-ach—if I read the Chinese mind accurately.

I was so weak that I wanted to lie down and die, but I forced myself to smile and eat. Mickey was glad for this close contact with the Chinese family, but he got on me for my lack of pres-ence on camera. He would say: "Stan, be yourself. You don't have to always be smiling!"

They had warned me that the shot would make me per-spire, and it did in fact. Thankfully, I also slept. I didn't lie awake long enough to become anxious about whether I could continue the run, or whether the next day I would be put in the hospital.

The following morning, a doctor came to give me an injec-tion of gluconate, but I figured I had risked enough. That fail-ing, he wrote out a prescription for more medicines. "You have to take a lot of tablets" (fifty-two to be exact), he as-sured me, waving off my fear of an overdose. "Chinese medi-cine is not so strong."

Obediently I took the tablets, not knowing what I was taking—wishing Hugo were there. Two days later I made note of what was happening to me:

> It is Sunday, October 28, and I am taking a rest break with Mickey and our old new friend, Mr. Chen. I have taken many Chinese herbs. There's no telling how many pills I have taken, but they have evidently done the trick because I am feeling like a wild bull today. I have run thirty-two kilometers before twelve o'clock. [I would run a total of sixty kilometers that day.]

That night I added a few more memories to the tape before I shut my eyes. By now, in many ways the days seemed to fade, one into the other. And the long road only opened up on more of the same—great crowds of onlookers, toiling farmers, and a hundred ways to have noodles.

> Today, in one of the vans there were four policemen, the head of a provincial ministry, and a doctor. The minister spoke fluent English and asked me, "Are you a Catholic?" I just looked at him, not knowing what to say. "No, but I am a Christian; I happen to go to a Baptist church." "Well," he said, "the doctor in the back, she wanted to know." At that I pulled the cross from under my shirt, and everyone applauded. "The doctor wants to study English," he said. I offered him a Bible for her, if she could receive it without causing any problem, and he assured me it would be all right. "I don't want to do anything inappropriate," I said. "Oh, it would be appropriate," he assured me. Then he said, "If you have two, I'd like one also." When we stopped, I couldn't run fast enough to get them from the wagon. I had brought some copies of a pocket-size New Testament with Psalms and Proverbs, and I opened that up to Proverbs, because it was familiar. Reading several of the verses from Proverbs Twenty-Eight, I could see he was very interested. In a while I resumed my running, and when the van passed, I saw everyone inside was huddled near the official who appeared to be reading from the Bible.

Lying in bed reflecting on the spiritual hunger among the Chinese, I silently thanked God for the opportunities He was giving me to give Bibles to some of the people. And I thought

of the words a pastor had written in my book of memories before I left the United States. Opening the book, I turned to the
place where he had written these words:

Stan,

> *Years upon years, each seemingly shorter than the one
> preceding, gather their memories one by one into an old
> scrapbook with delicate leaves—tears and laughter, trag-
> edy and triumph hidden among those pages, dog-eared
> from midnight perusals. When finally our scrapbooks
> close and we stand before God, brothers in Christ, I believe
> the little section marked China Run is going to receive a
> smile and a well done . . . because it was done for His
> kingdom.*

In Christ,
HUGH JOHNSON

Thousands of people had lined the roadway as I entered the
town that afternoon. Running with me were several Chinese
athletes. This part buoyed my spirits. I could not believe the
turnout they gave me. The streets were packed ten and
twelve deep, and they applauded.

"Zhong mei you hao wan cui," I would yell. "Long live the
friendship between China and the United States!" And they
would go wild. What a good feeling!

After supper we went across the street for a program the
city had planned for our benefit. There was Ping-Pong, and I
was impressed by the quickness and aggressiveness of even
the children. I was asked to play against an eight-year-old girl,
and I discovered she was better than most adults I've seen.
Mickey filmed this, as well as several minutes of a martial arts
demonstration.

When it came time for us to go to our lodging, the girl I had
played Ping-Pong with ran to my side, held my hand, and laid
her head over against my hand for a brief time. The look of enthusiasm and tenderness in those children's eyes touched
me. For all the times I had questioned why I came to China,
that brief encounter went a long way toward giving me the
answer.

By Monday, October 29, I had actually moved 17 kilometers ahead of schedule.

Leaving this village that had received us so warmly the previous evening, I agreed to a token run for the townspeople. I would run out of town and then return, in the company of several of their runners, before we proceeded on our way. After I had run about a kilometer and was returning, a lone woman broke away from the crowd and came running toward me. She had something in her hand—the distance was too great for me to tell what it was. Suddenly the police swarmed around her and dragged her away screaming. I never learned what she was attempting to do. But after that I didn't begrudge the protection the police gave me, although at times I thought they were a little too eager.

The police wore olive drab uniforms with a red flag on the collar, blue overcoats, and garrison caps proudly displaying a red star above the bill. Once, two people ran up to me with pens in their hands, wanting my autograph. But out of nowhere the police appeared, grabbed the paper out of the hands of these strangers and pulled me through the crowd.

In town after town the police literally had to go ahead of us and open up enough room for us to pass. Everyone wanted to see the *meigwo ren*. If this is what a president has to put up with all the time, I feel for him! I felt like a curiosity in a sideshow. And yet, at the same time, I couldn't deny the thrill that went through me, that so many people lined the road to see *me*—that Stan Cottrell was the first American some of these people had ever seen. Like they do a performer on stage, the crowds excited me and lifted my spirits.

And then, on November 2, Kevin arrived from Beijing, bringing me a telex. When I opened it, my eyes immediately caught the address of the sender: the White House. Kevin stood by as I read it aloud:

The Honorable Stan Cottrell

Dear Stan,
    Congratulations on your Friendship Run through China, from Beijing to Canton. As an avid jogger myself, I

know this special opportunity must mean a great deal.
Please know that we are all thinking of you at this time.

> *Sincerely,*
> *George Bush*
> *Vice-President*
> *The United States of America*

Wow! What a shot in the arm! Obviously, news of this traveled rapidly throughout our entourage. I don't think anything could have been as timely as this telex. In retrospect, I think my receiving it changed the overall outcome as far as the film studio's continuing with the filming after the November 15 deadline was concerned.

As for me, those few words reminded me of a trait I have in common with my mother. I remember that we used to work long hard days in the tobacco fields, and she would tell me that she didn't mind how hard she worked as long as somebody appreciated it. She also said that an encouraging word would make her work from sunup to sundown.

"Why, Lord, child, if I know somebody appreciates me I'll bust a hame string [a leather strap that goes around a horse, holding on the harness] working." Here was the vice-president of the United States saying, "Atta boy, Stanley junior—we're rootin' for you!" No amount of money could have bought or duplicated the feelings I had at that moment.

14

Oh, China!

For four days straight in early November we shook the hand of China's poverty—some of the nation's worst we were told. I don't say this demeaningly, for though the hand may be calloused and soiled, yet the face wears a smile.

China's peasants number some 800 million and since, under the "responsibility system," the government now allows its people to earn money on the side, their average income had risen to 310 yuan annually by the end of 1984. But that is a mere $117, about what our family spends on groceries a week! I've read that half a million peasants in the province of Hunan, farther south, subsist on less than a 100 yuan a year, and I don't doubt that many in the Yellow River region in Henan province, through which we now were passing, were equally as poor.

The flooded Yellow River (or Huang Ho) devastated this area regularly until a few years ago, so much so that the Yellow River has been called "China's Sorrow." One of the worst floods in recorded history, since the deluge of Noah's time, claimed 3.7 million people in 1931, and it happened along the Yellow River's plain.

The bridge across the river is narrow and repairs were being made on it the day we crossed. To prevent too many vehicles from being on the bridge at one time, guards were posted at either end. To the driver coming from one direction, a guard gave a stick of bamboo. He would proceed across the bridge, followed by the next forty-nine vehicles. The fiftieth carried a second stick of bamboo. When the first driver reached the other side, he would hand the guard there the bamboo stick, which would be given to the next car going across the bridge in the opposite direction after the fifty vehicles had all crossed. The fiftieth car would yield up its bamboo stick to the guard also, who would count fifty vehicles going in the opposite direction, and hand over the stick to the fiftieth driver.

Interestingly, we were not allowed to film my running across the bridge at the muddy Yellow River. Later, when in order to get a little of the local color we filmed a woman near the bridge, the police insisted on looking through the cameras to make sure that the bridge wasn't in view. We understood that they regarded the bridge as "sensitive" for internal security reasons, which seemed ludicrous to me in this age of satellite photography.

At the river's edge I accommodated the film crew by running along the bank of the river. Some fisherwomen were standing on the bank, and I stopped to shake hands with one of them. An old woman on the bank showed me several six-inch fish she had caught that day. Then she invited me inside the boat where she and her husband lived. It was crude but clean, with many pictures on the walls of the cramped quarters.

After crossing the Yellow River and passing through Kaifeng, we stopped for the night. The only thing that made the lodgings bearable was the bathhouse. We had fussed enough about needing a bath—I had, especially, after running all day. And I wasn't about to complain when we finally reached the bathhouse and found dirty water awaiting us. At least it was hot. I ignored the scum on the water as Mickey and I luxuriated for a while. The hot soaking relieved my aching, throbbing muscles.

My mattress that night listed about forty degrees to the left, so I brought in the pad from the *da puncha*. But I wasn't about to put it on the dirty floor to sleep, for fear of rats. Luckily I had some extra blankets; folding them beneath the left side of the mattress provided a fairly even surface for sleeping.

Taking precautions against the rats reminded me of our brief encounter that morning with the "rat man." We had stopped at a roadside market, where merchants were practicing a little private enterprise. One was a "dentist" who pulled teeth for one yuan (thirty-five cents) and displayed at least three dozen of them on a table. Not far away was a talkative gentleman holding two dead rats by the tail as nonchalantly as if they were coon tails. Several more specimens lay on the table before him while he hawked his specialty—rat poison. He guaranteed—100 percent—no more rats; one sniff and they would die! I wondered how he could handle those poisoned rats and in the next breath take a drink of tea, and suffer no ill effect.

"He says the poison does no harm to humans," Mickey assured me. I wasn't going to question his word.

The next night's lodging proved to be even worse. Cracks in the window let in the cold night air, relieving somewhat the sickening smells. The place was a firetrap. It reeked of gasoline, and exposed wiring hung from the ceiling. I looked outside our second-floor window to see if I could leap to safety in the event of a fire, and just as I did, someone from the floor above emptied a pan of water right over the window.

As I lay in bed that night, too weary to defend myself

against all the imagined predators lurking in the dark, I wondered if this building had served as a prison compound in the revolution, or during World War II. It looked for all the world like such a place. I was glad we were moving on in the morning.

I really didn't mind sharing the lot of the common man; seeing and smelling and tasting China was what lured me here. I've never been one for luxurious tours. Nevertheless I was looking forward to the comforts of the international hotel Grace promised was up ahead.

The peasant knows nothing of a ritzy hotel. In Henan Province, many appeared to be living in caves dug out of the hills. I now understand that some thousands along the river are living this way temporarily because they are being relocated out of flood plains and are building their houses. This may have been the case in Henan Province. I don't know. Most of the houses in this area were of straw and mud, with dirt floor and small windows.

In this part of China we kept seeing mounds of dirt in the fields; these, we learned, were graves. In the country, the people bury their dead above ground and then cover them over (in the cities, cremation is the required method). During the Cultural Revolution, probably in an attempt to erase the past, the people had to remove all the grave markers, but some have now begun to reappear.

One day early in November the local officials arranged for us to meet a young couple who were to be married. Mickey and I wanted to present them with some gift, but didn't know what we could give them. We finally settled on a large bag of puffed rice. We had gotten this rice a few days earlier after watching a man in one village puffing the rice with an old-fashioned hand-cranked machine that looked more like a cannon than a rice popper. He would turn the crank for five minutes at least and then strike the machine with an iron tool, setting off an explosion. Out would pop the puffed rice into a large cotton bag!

The newlyweds invited us to their wedding and allowed us

to film a part of it. To one side of the room where they were to be married was the room where they would spend their honeymoon, and we were shown into it. On a wall and on a simple chest at least ten baby pictures were displayed! These, I learned, were for good luck, representing the wishes of friends and family that a healthy baby would grace this new couple's home. Of course, China officially discourages its families from having more than one child.

Down the road, at the crest of a small hill, was a factory where porcelain caskets were built. The factory had a most-novel feature. Whenever someone selected a coffin, it was placed in a sort of chute and sent skimming down the hill to where the new owner would load it on a cart and take it away. Mickey and I couldn't help ourselves—to think that coffins would ride down the chute like so many logs in an adventure-park flume, struck us as hilarious. We had to film it. But that proved to be in poor taste. Members of our film crew persuaded us that to do so would bring bad luck to the bridal couple. And besides, it would be wrong to film happiness and follow that by such a symbol of sadness.

I will say one thing for the Chinese. They keep their dirt clean! Every morning they are out sweeping the area around their homes, and they do it in the evening also, even if the neighbor is preparing a meal outside. The average Chinese must consume several ounces of dirt a day. What we would call roadside inns were always right on the edge of the road. I wouldn't have believed it had I not seen it. Meals were being prepared and eaten not far from where trucks and carts passed with their trailing cloud of dust.

The dust bothered my running more than any other element. You can dress for the cold and the rain, but you can't keep from breathing in the dirt. Every attempt to clear the throat brings up ugly black sputum. Meanwhile, the nostrils get all clogged up and quit working altogether. Along this part of the run I fought for breath desperately and had to slow my pace so that my lungs could get enough air.

Depression plagued me in this setting—not only because of the squalor, but because I could not eat the food. My weight was getting dangerously low. On leaving America, I had weighed a pudgy 149 pounds—the heaviest I have ever weighed—but now I was down to 136. I couldn't afford to lose more than another 4 pounds—yet I couldn't eat. For days I went around feeling nauseous. I wouldn't try the soups because I knew that they were concocted with the foul water. And I figured if I couldn't get the food past my nose, my stomach wasn't going to take to it very well. I hated to be this way, for the Chinese were giving us their best, and we didn't want to offend them. One night I ate nothing but a few peanuts. The only drink served, besides the dingy tea, was *pijiu,* a beer. I ate nuts and took a few swallows of beer. Not exactly a high-carbohydrate diet for long-distance running!

Grace saved the day more than once by fixing me a tasty, nutritious lunch. On the day that I "feasted" on peanuts and beer, she prepared a delicious fruit salad. And she brought me some bottled mineral water to wash it down with; another day she made me a spinach broth with some boiled mineral water.

All along I was counting on Hugo's joining me, but when by the third of November it appeared impossible to cover his expenses, I told Carol to go ahead and ship my nutritional supplies to me. Yet that was small consolation. I figured that the supplies would be more than three weeks reaching me— and the run would be over in five weeks. If I could keep running.

I had completely recovered from the flu, but not before passing it on to Mickey. Actually, I think his difficulties with the Beijing Film Studio had more to do with his becoming sick than whatever bug I had. Mickey knew that he was "my" director, but Mr. Du didn't know that. Barely ten days into the run I saw this entry in Mickey's notes:

Relations with Mr. Du have grown so bad that I am having no influence on the film. He is shooting things in an awkward newsreel sort of style and creating a film that would possibly please a Chinese audience, but this would be thought very corny by the . . . American audience. Saturday night I was becoming ill and told Stan that unless something changed it was useless for me to continue. This upset Stan.

The problems were so severe that I talked with Mr. Du and Mrs. Shr, one of the best camera operators on the crew, and told them that if Mickey quit that would be the end of the film. For a time, that seemed to return the reins to Mickey's hands, but only because Du's boss was then traveling with us. When this man left, Mickey's headaches with Du resumed. Probably, Du found himself in an uncomfortable position. He had been given a position of responsibility by the film service for which he had neither the training nor the command of English. No doubt this explained some of his behavior—but that didn't make it any easier for Mickey.

To make it easier for Mickey to create visually cohesive scenes without my wearing a different wardrobe each time, we decided I would dress in a different color of clothing in each province, and wear only that color while running until we reached the next provincial border.

In Henan, I was wearing blue shorts with a blue long-sleeve top. On November 5 the journey took us beside a very picturesque canal and Mickey naturally wanted to capture me and my reflection in the water. What we didn't count on was the squishy soil and the overpowering stench coming from that lazy canal. I suddenly ran kneedeep and fell face forward in mud and manure and fairly messed up my entire outfit. I was a pathetic sight! But Mickey loved it—this was the unexpected that added just what he was after. Hadn't he told me only the day before, "Stan, most of all, let's get your pain and hardship on camera"? He was getting it.

I was cold and shivering. Here were hundreds of Chinese coming out of nowhere to look at this strange spectacle. Seeing me looking like a mud ball, a woman offered to wash my running pants in the river. But the police kept driving her back. Mickey understood the woman's Chinese and at his insistence they let me stop and shed the dirty gear so she could wash the pants in the river.

I do not know what moved her to do that, but it was typical of the way strangers were treating us as we moved through their land. She didn't have a meal to offer me, or flowers—but she gave me a gift of her kindness. I offered her money but she refused it. Grace interpreted what the woman said: "Why would he want to give me money for washing his clothes?" The touch of that woman's deed stayed with me throughout that day—and longer.

As for paying the woman, since tipping is not allowed, even in city restaurants, I suppose I put her in an awkward position by offering her money.

Other little things helped dispel the drudgery of the seven-day-a-week routine we were into, like the Voice of America broadcast on November 5. It made us feel a little nearer home. The news that night was that President Reagan was favored to win the election the next day by a landslide.

Like most Americans I think nothing of wearing a different outfit each day. But not so the Chinese. Grace wore the same pants and blouse, I believe, every day we were on the run. Even Mr. Chen, when he was with us for five or six days, always wore the same outfit. I do not think they did this only from choice. A few hundred yuan do not go very far.

Silver linings did lighten the gray sameness of these days of running . . . running. For one thing, I was running strong now. Ten or 20 kilometers went by much easier than at the start when I was trying to get back in shape. For another, sometimes Mickey and I were allowed to walk about in the town where we stayed. We took that as a vote of confidence. We never saw any other Caucasians on those strolls, and we were told that we were the first Caucasians many of these people had seen. When we entered a shop, they would stop what they were doing and stare at us in silence. It was next to impossible for Mickey to direct any filming in these settings, for he had a real problem with crowd control. The people would follow us around and gather by the score in the entryway of shops. Mickey looked for spontaneity, for ways to let the camera somehow become an unobtrusive, inconspicuous recorder. But he couldn't do this much of the time since the film crew were not trained in that method. And whenever the lights were turned on and the little clapper board routine carried out, everyone obviously stiffened up!

Traveling throughout the countryside we observed that the people were wakened each morning by loudspeakers. Promptly at 6:30 A.M. the news went on, and all China, it seemed, roused out of sleep. This was repeated each evening at 7:30. The people stood around to hear the "town crier" give the news, and to read what appeared on bulletin boards. Then virtually everyone disappeared. I suppose they went to bed. The regimentation struck us as one of the most difficult of the constraints on these people.

When we were lodged in the factories and in occasional communes, we were never afraid that we would miss a meal. The people are called to the dining hall by a loud clang-clang on an iron bar outside the door. And seeing the people drop everything and head for the hall reminded me of suppertime on the farm. Whatever you were doing, you dropped it and came a-running. The Chinese didn't run to the dining hall, but they never had to be called twice!

On November 7 Radio Moscow, broadcasting in English, filled the air with propaganda. I had heard of these broadcasts, but until I listened myself I never imagined they twisted the truth quite so much as they do. What garbage they spew out! That night the Voice of America appeared to be jammed a lot, but we did get the news that Reagan was ahead in every state except Wisconsin with 80 percent of the votes in.

Earlier that day I fell into conversation with a Mr. Zhong, a translator with the China Sports Service Company. He was asking about America, and about what made me run. This led to a discussion of my values. For once no crowd was pressing me; he seemed interested in the Bible so I showed him mine and read a few verses for him. Turning to John 3:16 I read:

> For God so loved the world, that he gave his only be-gotten Son, that whosoever believeth in him should not perish, but have everlasting life.

Then I told him he could put his name in that statement, like this:

> For God so loved (Mr. Zhong) that he gave his only begotten Son, that if (Mr. Zhong) believeth in him, (Mr. Zhong) shall not perish, but have everlasting life.

"If you want to have eternal life and be forgiven your sins, just tell Jesus you want Him to come into your life," I said.

That evening before I turned out the light, he came to my room to talk more. As I drifted off to sleep, I felt that I could see some overarching purpose in this run. My heart was full as I thanked God for a roof over my head and for allowing me to talk to people about Him.

That night the rains came.

15

The Long Middle of the Journey

"If I don't complete this run, the Chinese will think I'm just some flake, Mickey."

"I know."

"And I'm serious when I say *if*. In six days I've got to have $50,000 for the Beijing Film Studio, and if I don't have it, I don't know what might happen to us. I still remember what David Aikman told me: 'The Chinese are hard to figure out. One day they are your best friend. But the next day they can be your deadly enemy.' "

As serious as the money problem appeared, it was actually dwarfed by the difficulties now developing with the filming. After twenty-two days the film studio was still doing their own thing. Daily Mickey would come to me with impossibly sticky situations. At least one member of the film crew told Mickey that, basically, the crew themselves did not trust Mr. Du. They believed he felt no responsibility at all to Mickey or me—this, even though the same person said Du had been instructed by his superiors to cooperate and shoot exactly what Mickey wanted.

Thankfully, Kevin arrived and arranged to meet with both sides to seek a resolution. Mickey made notes from that meeting:

> I pointed out that the theme was about Stan running long distance. Du would shoot staged (crowd clapping) scenes and athletes signing book and then posing, exchanges at bridges with police [which are] boring. I emphasized that shooting of these things with our precious film was driving Stan crazy. . . . Du only perceived this as an ego-type confrontation. . . .

Heading the list of Mickey's requirements was that he be allowed to perform the duties of producer and director. Mr. Du, after all, was totally unfamiliar with the intended American audience. Various points of the contract were being violated; others were being changed without prior agreement. Kevin listened and counseled patience.

The next day, a crew member confided to Mickey that the film studio had held "an important meeting" the previous night. Interestingly, Mickey and I were excluded from these meetings. At that meeting, Mr. Du had criticized one of the camera operators for shooting scenes of Stan without instructions from him. Two members of the film crew decided to go on strike because of Du's action, and the operator had subsequently gone to Du to complain about his making his criticism in front of the others. With all of this turmoil spinning around in Mickey's ears, he came to me the next day and expressed serious doubts that we could successfully complete the film. Mickey's notes again:

> His [my] immediate reaction was that there would be no more shooting that day. . . . The crew was as-

tounded. The rest of the day I walked with Stan. He
was very upset and depressed. Every time Du would
pass he would glare at us. . . . Stan wanted to send me
to Beijing to meet with the United States embassy and
with the heads of Beijing Film. Grace said that we
weren't near the railroad but that she would call Mr.
Chen in Beijing. Stan remained firm. He had really
lost his running spirit and was miserable. . . .

The response to Grace's call was that Kevin and Mr. Chen
would come to a meeting in Wuhan, now five days ahead of
us. We would hash everything out then. Being in no mood to
run, I resisted that. We needed to talk it out now, if we could.

The following morning, in Shin Tsai, Mickey came to my
room and found me with Mr. Du, Grace, Mrs. Shr, and Lea, a
girl who operated the sound equipment. We had heard Du
shouting over the phone to someone the previous night. We
wondered if he had received a dressing down, for now he was
finally acting halfway civil. That morning was the first in-
stance in which either Mickey or I heard him acknowledge
that some of the film crew had criticized him for not coop-
erating with us. He also said that some members of the crew
were saying false things about him behind his back. That little bit of give on Du's part allowed us to find a new ground of
cooperation.

Mickey joked with me once in a while about my
"speeches"—but it was time for one at that session. I recall
telling Mr. Du and the others, "This is an extraordinary
event. It calls for extraordinary courage and patience. We
must forget ourselves. For this run to succeed, we must step
outside of ourselves and work for the common good." I meant
every word.

Mr. Du, having lost some face, agreed to try to be more
agreeable.

That rainy day fit our moods. We got a late start, but by
mid-morning we were pushing on down the road. We stopped
once and as I stood in the protection of a shed, I explained

some of the problems of running in the rain, while Mickey directed the filming.

In the evening, the local mayor and his official guests hosted a dinner in our honor, and I was happy to see that members of the film crew were trying to smooth things out. Mrs. Kahn, who served as sort of a managerial liaison for the studio, who is normally very quiet, made toasts to both Mickey and me, wishing for cooperation and success. I spoke to the assembled group, extemporizing as I normally do.

"I hope that this run will help bring our two countries a little closer together, that the ocean of distance between us will shrink a little because of our efforts. But you cannot do it alone, and neither can I. All of you are making it happen. Every person is a link in the chain."

Later that night, Mickey said that my remarks were just right for a Marxist audience! I had told them what they are always saying—everyone together doing the needed thing. No wonder they cheered me so!

The filming and the run were definitely taking their toll on Mickey. He was also missing his family, as was I. The financial bind wore on both of us. But we couldn't afford to feel sorry for ourselves.

Despite the pressures, Mickey had not lost the edge in his professional directing. His advice to me, when on camera, included the following:

1. Try not to talk in generalities. Be specific.
2. Be light and easy most of the time.
3. Remember to breathe.
4. Separate yourself from yourself, and watch yourself.
5. Don't hesitate to laugh.
6. Don't talk so loud.
7. Remember, you are talking to one person and not to a crowd.
8. If Mickey interrupts, don't get mad. Take a deep breath and start again.
9. Don't say Mickey's name (when answering a question).
10. Don't talk in past or future tense unless Mickey asks

you; some of the footage may be used in different
places in the film.
   11. Think Elvis—"Hey baby!" (a gimmick to get me to
   relax).

We were running in the "long middle" of the journey.
Gone was the excitement of the start and the newness of the
run. Guangzhou, our destination in one month, seemed as far
away as the other side of the world.

Each evening Mickey and I performed a small ritual, which
we looked forward to eagerly. Sitting in the gypsy wagon, we
would take a pen and draw an X through another day on the
homemade calendar on the wall. How the days dragged by.
The finish looked an eternity away.

Day after day clouds obscured the skies, shutting out
the sun, making each day seem without beginning or end.
Slap, slap went my weary feet on the dusty road. To relieve the
tight muscles in my upper arms and neck, I would raise my
hands high above my head and run that way. Or I would let
my arms dangle at my sides awhile, like the legs of a stuffed
doll.

The rains that fell during these days actually stimulated me
though they slowed our progress. Running long distances requires something of the mind as well as the body. I think running is even more of a mental chore than a physical one. The
mind must have something to concentrate on, something to
work on, or else the body's pains will force the distance runner to quit. And I was having pain enough. Every day a knife
seemed to turn in my side, starting in the morning and lasting
all day long. Muscles in my groin would twitch and my back
would feel at times as if it would break. But with the rains
came puddles and suddenly I would forget my agony and
begin to think of how I could time my steps to skip over the
little puddles that were forming. It became a game. I started
counting to see how many steps I could take before encountering another puddle. 1 . . . 2 . . . 3 . . . Leap. 1 . . . 2 . . . 3 . . .
4 . . . 5. I went all the way to 25 before I tired of that game.
Slap, slap, slap, *leap*. Since I was a little boy again—in my

imagination, a Chinese lad out for a spree—I could indulge the child's bent for running *in* the water. I could not resist it when a shallow puddle came up. Slap, slap, slap, slap, *splash*. Running through the showers and leaping over little ponds, I was getting on down the road. Kilometers flew by when this was my game.

More than once as the weary days mounted, the situation reminded me of Hugo's words when I was on the verge of quitting the run through Europe. I had been running seventy days and was burned out, talking of stopping.

"Go ahead and quit," he said. "You're the only one who will suffer the embarrassment!"

I wondered how he could be so cold, so unfeeling toward me. But now I understood that he had to be, and Mickey and I had to be tough on each other—or we would never make it.

I didn't feel particularly tough, however.

The deadline for the money hung heavy over my head. And in talking with Carol I learned that we had exhausted all our potential leads for raising funds. We had hit zero. One assuring thing she did say was that our need for funds, and the run itself, was to go before the congregation at our home church the following Sunday. The people would be praying. We needed a miracle.

"Read Psalm 91, Stan," Carol said. It was probably all she felt she had to offer—but it was the kind of help I needed. That night I turned to that Psalm, and saw immediately why she had suggested it.

> He that dwelleth in the secret place of the most High shall abide under the shadow of the Almighty. I will say of the Lord, He is my refuge and my fortress: my God; . . . he shall give his angels charge over thee, to keep thee in all thy ways. They shall bear thee up in their hands, lest thou dash thy foot against a stone. . . . He shall call upon me, and I will answer him: I will be with him in trouble; I will deliver him, and honour him (Psalms 91:1, 2, 11, 12, 15).

I didn't underestimate the heavy load she was carrying at home. Stanley III and Michelle were definitely hurting because of my being away, and they were getting along about as happily as any normal teenagers. Which means they were feuding, and Carol had her hands full.

Little Jennifer, bless her heart, had told me on the phone: "Daddy, please quit and come home."

She promised to write and did so, but her letter never reached me in China. One day in February 1985 the postman delivered it to our home in Georgia; it had traveled all the way to Beijing, to Guangzhou, and back home in Georgia. I still opened it with eager anticipation.

> *Dear Daddy,*
> *I hope you are feeling better. Hope you are doing good.*
> *I wish you would quit and come home. I love you*
> *sooooooo much. Write me back.*
>
> > *Love,*
> > *Jenny*

Talking to Jenny and knowing what burdens Carol bore just tore me up. But somehow, she kept calm. She had been so strong during the past year, and her strength rubbed off on me, halfway around the world.

Her faith in me persisted despite what others back home were saying. Once she told me that a neighbor said, of me: "Well, I hope he knows what he's doing. I hope he is accomplishing something." That day I had just had one of the greatest thrills of the China run. A crowd of 2,000 people had waited almost eight hours to see me pass, and I had been toasted that evening at a banquet by a local official who said sincerely, "This is truly a unique gesture of friendship. This will be written in the history of this province."

The next day Mickey wanted to film me running through one of the villages. It had seemed like a good idea. And I was in an accommodating mood, for on the previous day we had traveled through a forty-mile stretch of road where no one had been allowed to take even a snapshot, let alone movie footage. We imagined security was the reason.

Mickey thought this particular village would serve as a fitting backdrop for the run, but we failed to take one thing into account—the rains had turned the streets into quicksand. I was being careful, but the manure-laden muck was too slippery and I went facedown in the cold yukky slop. At least we got it on film. Grace rushed me to a place where I could change clothes and stick my feet in hot water, for the weather had turned cold. Thankfully, I did not get sick again, but I was almost too sick of spirit to put up with any more. My nerves were shot and my emotions ran the gamut—from runner's high, to extreme feelings of loneliness, to despair.

Once that day Mickey came along beside me while I was running and shouted, "What's happened? Is something wrong?" Tears were streaming down my face. I just shook my head.

I had been reflecting on the vivid dream I had had that morning just prior to waking. In my dream, Daddy appeared before me. I said, "Daddy, is that you?"

And he answered, "Yes, Son. For the last five years you have been calling and calling!

"Come here, Son," Daddy said, and he put his arms around me. I felt his strength—the security and comfort of being close to him was so real. And he said, "Son, I never said it when I could have, but I love you." I was crying. He looked so wonderful. It seemed as if we talked for hours; it was a very happy time. Then he said, "I have to leave now." I was in the phase of not wanting to wake up, in limbo between the dream world and the first drowsy glimpse of morning. I awoke crying so hard that my eyes were puffy, as though I had been in a fistfight.

That night David Mah, an American citizen living in Beijing, who exercises some influence among the Chinese, tried to encourage me.

"Stan, you are the diplomat. God has chosen you for this

fifty-day run through China." I didn't know about that; all I was doing was trying to run one day at a time. And no way would his words get me puffed up, not after what I was running in and falling in day after day, and sleeping in night after night. But his call did help me.

On November 10 we crossed into Hubei Province (Hupeh on older maps) and caught our first glimpse of rice paddies and abundant green foliage. We were averaging about forty miles a day and now, after three weeks, we had reached the semitropical zone. We were about as far south as the Georgia-Florida state line, and the terraced mountains gave a scenic beauty to the land. In this province I wore a blue warm-up suit, and, on most days, my stocking cap and gloves. Two days after entering the province, Mickey and I knew (almost to the very minute) when we reached the official halfway point in the run. It was in the provincial capital, Wuhan, a metropolis of 4.5 million people, the largest industrialized city in central China. Astride the mighty Yangtze in a misty, cold rain, Wuhan gave us our long-anticipated stay in the international hotel—a wonderful tonic for my spirits.

Also in Wuhan the Sports Service brought me cases of wonderful bottled Looshan Springs mineral water and stored them in the gypsy wagon. It was delicious in contrast to the regular water. From then on I never needed to worry about my water supply.

Grace and Mr. Mee, another of the drivers, continued to boil and filter water from Shag's plastic jug, and use it for washing and cooking. Mr. Mee helped with some of the kitchen chores in the van. We called him "Big Bear" because he must have stood six feet two and weighed over 200 pounds, and also because he had with him in the car two little stuffed panda bears. He carried on over those toy bears as a child would have. Grace knitted a jacket for each one, and Mr. Mee talked about it for days.

In the hotel I luxuriated in the first hot bath I'd had in at least two weeks; yet that was no greater cause for wonder than the rug on the floor. I've never stood and admired a floor rug as much I did the one in that room.

As refreshing as our stay in the hotel was, our lodging two nights earlier proved more memorable.

As they did everywhere we were received for lodging, the local authorities bowed and apologized overmuch for the meager facilities they offered us. My room was very plain. A low bed, with sheet and blanket, and an overstuffed chair, were the only furniture. They had swept the floor and wiped the gray walls, and while I was "moving in," an attendant walked in briskly and hung a "curtain" in the small window. It was a square of cotton print that reminded me of the feed sacks Momma used to make shirts for me and my brother, Harold, when we were in elementary school.

Along the wall about six feet high, a line could plainly be seen on the plaster. Probably the place had been under water in an earlier flood.

They were offering me their very best. What they could not offer was any heat because government policy forbade the use of heat until November 15. Interesting! I went to bed that night wearing sweat clothes and a green army overcoat like those worn by the People's Liberation Army.

Before resuming the run the following morning, I discovered a small garden next to the building where we stayed. Near the garden an open door revealed an empty room where stood a large conference table and several chairs; the place looked formal, museumish. It turned out that I had happened onto a bit of history, for in that room in 1949, I was told, General George C. Marshall's aide had met Premier Chou En-lai for some sort of talks.

Explaining the history to me was the gentlest young woman I met in all of China. Miss Dong Lee, a cook in the commune, seemed the epitome of Chinese grace. She was dressed plainly in brown pants, a sweater, and a brown coat. I will never forget her eyes. Her hands were calloused and hard as a carpenter's hands. She seemed to trust Mickey and me immediately; she wasn't reserved or shy.

I wanted to give her something and so I offered her a T-shirt. She expressed her appreciation genuinely and then hurried off to return with a ball-point pen which became her gift to me. Then she kissed my hand to say good-bye, an uncharacteristic gesture.

This young woman may spend her entire life in that commune. I could not tell if every field of endeavor is open to women in China today, but I observed no obvious discrimination against women. They hold responsible jobs in the People's Liberation Army and on the Beijing film crew, and I met several in professional positions while traveling through China. But also, everywhere I went, I saw women and young girls carrying huge loads. I remember seeing women as well as men inching along the city streets, under heavy burdens, straining to pull a loaded cart.

One night to my surprise a peasant girl came to my room. In broken English and with hand gestures she told me that the provincial authorities had sent her.

She said, "You are *lao shr* [teacher]."

"What do you want?" I asked her.

"I want to learn English," she said.

"I am not a good worker," she continued, expressing herself with some difficulty. It turned out that she worked in the hotel dining hall, from six in the morning until nine at night, six days a week. It was 9:05 when she came to my room.

"The governor of our province said that you are a teacher, and you can teach me."

In Chinese society, I was learning, nothing is worse than to be regarded as a nonproducer, a parasite. I thought the governor was to be commended for encouraging her to improve herself.

She was about twenty-five, small, with a troubled face—not unattractive, but definitely unhappy. I learned that she was unmarried and had no boyfriend.

"I am ugly," she said shamefacedly, the thought evidently prompted by her revelation that she had no boyfriend. "I am not a worker. I have no skill. . . . No boy wants me."

Normally at that hour I was already asleep, but class immediately commenced! I invited several people who were standing around to join us for an English lesson.

Drawing an *A,* I said to her, "This is the letter *A.*"

"This is *A,*" she said.

Then she drew the letter.

"This is the letter *B,*" I continued. Each time I introduced a letter, she would repeat it after me and draw it on the notebook paper she had brought with her. She seemed bright enough, and she stayed right with me for almost an hour. For each letter of the alphabet, I had her draw a picture of something beginning with that letter. Then I would ask her to teach me the Chinese word for the object she drew.

"The word *apple* starts with *A,*" I told her, and she seemed to understand. *Apple* in English, *pinggwo* in Chinese. It was fun, but finally my eyeballs couldn't focus, I was so bone tired.

"I'm tired," I confessed, and so "class" recessed. I think everyone would have stayed all night. They were all hungry for knowledge and hung on every word I said.

"I am ugly," the girl had said. "I am not a worker . . . no skill. . . . No boy wants me." What this girl was saying revealed a great deal about family ideals in China. If it does not make economic sense for a fellow and a girl to marry, then they don't! Emotions, looks, and the superficial factors we in America use as guidelines for choosing a life partner are secondary in China to one thing: How good a worker are you and what is your skill? I felt that the Chinese understand better than the Westerner that love is not an emotion, but an act of the will. "I choose to love you," they might say, "to marry you—because you are capable of pulling your load right along beside me!"

16

A Church in Changsha

Day 28 of the run brought us through more rain. The showers felt like a thousand peppering needles against my face. But I didn't mind running in the misty rain; the water made the road surface spongy and the cool water felt invigorating to my skin. I think a car motor runs more efficiently in the rain, and the same can be said for the human "motor." At least that's the way it is with me. Obviously, the cooler the temperature, the less heat the body will produce.

Yet this posed another problem. In my running gear, I was sweating like a chicken trying to lay a goose egg, and had no way to ventilate my clothing. I must have stopped a dozen times that day to change shirts. If I hadn't done that, I would have gotten a chill, especially with my low body fat. By the end of the day wet clothes hung everywhere inside the *da puncha* and that night I asked Grace to please do whatever was necessary to dry my shirts by morning—even if a couple of the people had to fan them all night long.

Under ordinary circumstances the China Sports people would wash my clothes for me every few days, but with no clothes dryers, they would be dripping wet when returned the next day. This time I couldn't afford to begin the day with wet clothes, for even though we were moving south, we were also encountering freezing temperatures. There were reports of snow in Beijing and a cold front was rapidly catching up with us. Ahead lay the mountains.

That night, heat was permitted in our building—another first for the trip. But I was denied that small comfort. When I entered the room assigned to me, five men were standing on my bed, looking at the air conditioner mounted on the wall. Evidently it was a new installation, although it looked to me to be twenty-five years old at least. They were turning the knobs and talking excitedly, trying to find the heat control, all the while oblivious to the fact that atop a bed might seem a strange place for the five of them to be standing, especially since the "occupant" had just entered the room. The contraption proved to be as stubbornly inscrutable to them as their language remained to me. I finally assured them that I had done without heat so far and could get by that night without heat also.

Some heat would have been nice, for the cold would not let up. And our overnight quarters were not to improve immediately. I remember one night, sitting on my bed, after my "bath," clad in sweat clothes, socks, and stocking cap, while Mickey held his hands up to a bare light bulb to catch what heat he could. Before that he went up and down the hall closing windows and doors. The outside temperature must have been near freezing, but the Chinese showed consistent indifference about shutting windows and doors.

When a member of China Sports happened by the room where Mickey and I were to sleep that night, Mickey called out to him, "Can you bring a water buffalo into the building tonight?"

The man stood and looked at us, trying to be sure he had heard Mickey correctly.

"A what?"

"A water buffalo. A cow. We would like a cow in our room tonight, okay?"

The man didn't know what to say. Frowning, he asked again, "Say it one more time, please?"

I joined in the fun. "He said we want a water buffalo in our room tonight," looking at the man as seriously as I knew how. "They are warm. We are not from a cold climate and we need it to stay warm. We don't mind cleaning up after it if you could get us one."

"Could we buy one for the night?"

By now the man seemed to understand the nature of our request. Remaining as serious as a mortician he muttered something I could not understand and went on his way.

The comedy made me think. Hadn't the Chinese promised us "the great ox"? I had come to China on that first visit with such high hopes. I was sure that dozens of America's energetic corporations would jump at the chance to support The Great Friendship Run in exchange for an opportunity to do business here. With solid support behind us we would bring our own film crew, and Hugo, and a still photographer; and my family would fly over for the finish in Guangzhou. But none of that had panned out. Instead of offering American businesses the great ox, I had succeeded in convincing only a few. It was hard not to be disappointed.

I knew my nerves were wearing thin and my tolerances weren't what they would normally be. But I continued to be baffled by the habit of the Chinese of changing their minds and never telling anybody. If they believe you will think less of them because they changed their minds, they will fail to mention the change. I reasoned that it had to do with saving face. I found myself wondering if this puzzling trait has hampered the Chinese in their trade negotiations with other nations. It surely played havoc with Mickey's relationship with the film crew. We also found thirty minutes of haggling to be the norm whenever we requested something.

Yet I reminded myself: *It's a miracle that I'm here, and that I'm running. I can endure anything for another twenty-five days.*

But I figured I had better not say that; I had already endured things I never dreamed I would.

The miracle continued. On November 14 Carol told me that $25,000—half of what was due the next day—had come in from one investor. It was his second large investment.

We were approaching people with what we considered a viable venture—asking them to help underwrite the cost of the film and share in the profits. Lois, Mickey's wife, was spending hours on the phone, searching for new investors. Everything about the run and the filming and the welcome China was giving us made me confident that these investors would not be disappointed—but it was difficult to convey that back home.

Carol shared other heartening news. Her phone was ringing twenty times a day with people calling to say they were praying for the run and for our family, and to express their concern. A couple in our Sunday school class had given her $500, and another man—whom I know could not afford it— gave her $250 to help her meet expenses.

I went to bed that night, buoyed by the dedication of our small team back home. But I teetered on the brink of despair. I had not made a penny so far and neither I nor anyone else knew where the other $25,000 was coming from, or if we could continue should the money not come in right away. I couldn't see a way through it all, but I couldn't quit either. It was hard to keep from getting discouraged. *Don't get bitter,* I told myself. *Get better. Get better . . . not bitter . . . better. God has us here for a reason. He works all things for good.*

Two days passed without any word from the film studio about the film payment. Everything continued as usual, so I assumed the rest of the money had come in. I was expecting at any time to learn that the money had arrived by wire in Beijing. Three days passed. Four days. . . .

On the night of November 18, our first night in Hunan province, Mickey arranged for some filming in our room. I was to ask Mr. Du some questions on camera. *Interesting,* I thought.

"China has an open-door policy," Mr. Du started. "You can say anything you want here. But you have not asked many questions. You perhaps would like to know something about our country and our customs—about anything? No? Please ask anything you like."

What he said surprised me. I am usually full of questions, but in China I clammed up. I think it was in order to avoid politics and, not knowing their culture, trying to be careful not to offend them. Du's question helped me relax a bit.

Since I could not even recall seeing men and women holding hands, I asked if men and women may show affection publicly.

"Maybe they hold hands behind closed doors in their bedroom," Mr. Du said.

I laughed at that reply.

I asked about birth control in China, to which I received a brief straightforward response. China has a policy: one child per family. Each province has birth-control programs, he said; the pill is provided. Beyond that, he would not elaborate.

I also asked about freedom of religion. "May I pray with another person if I wish? Is that permitted?"

Mr. Du said, "In the new China, you can be anything you want to be—a Christian, a Buddhist, a Muslim, an atheist—anything. No problem."

"And could an evangelist come to China and stay for a year and hand out Bibles? Would that be possible in China?"

That last question threw Mr. Du and his staff. It was evidently a hot potato, for they never did come up with an answer. They replayed the tape and listened to it over and over. Mickey didn't care for this format for the film—it was ridiculously contrived, stiff. But it seemed to be the only way we could include certain sensitive subjects in the filming.

Early in the run I began asking Grace to feed me potatoes. I explained to her how good a source of carbohydrates they are, and that I needed lots of them.

"They will help me keep my body weight," I told her. "Besides, I like potatoes." At that time I weighed 128 pounds.

"But potatoes are the food of the peasants."

"That doesn't bother me. Please get me potatoes."

She listened, but still I got no potatoes. Instead, they were serving me food that I couldn't eat.

One day I said to her, "Grace, does it mean if you feed me potatoes you will lose face?"

"Yes, I think so," she said.

"Well, if I don't get some potatoes soon, I will die and then everyone will *really* lose face!"

That got their attention, and Mickey and I were treated to fried potatoes. I thanked Grace and she must have passed the word to the cook—"He likes potatoes. Give him plenty."

I had forgotten all about it when we went to breakfast the following morning; but the cooks had not. We had eggs and fried potatoes—a poor excuse for grits for a Southern man—and I thanked Grace again. That evening for supper we had more fried potatoes. I should have known to expect this because earlier in the run when I had shown an interest in eggs, I got them three times a day. I got my fill of potatoes before they realized that I could get by once in a while without them.

The same thing happened with mushrooms. When they served us uncooked ones, I declined because I didn't think they would be safe for me. But I made the mistake of telling Grace that I did like mushrooms and that they would be good for me. For a whole week I think we had mushrooms at every meal, cooked in every conceivable way. One night we had eight different dishes of mushrooms. We even had mushroom cake!

"Anything you like, they keep pouring it on," Mickey observed. "And if you don't eat it, they think you don't like them."

Although sometimes disconcerting, the element of surprise can add zest to the day's events—even if such experiences have a zany quality to them. One evening Mickey and I were enjoying some *moli hwa cha* and savoring delicious fried chicken that Grace had prepared. The camera crew must have been enjoying it too, for they were making all sorts of smacking noises and spitting bones out on their plates.

"Is it possible to have more chicken?" I asked.

With an "I'll see," Grace got up and went back to the kitchen. I figured she was checking on the supply and when she returned nodding yes, I anticipated it being brought right away.

We went on talking and hardly noticed when a man walked through our dining area holding two live chickens by the feet. They lunged and fluttered just as he passed our table. He disappeared into the kitchen and we went on with our conversation. The next thing we heard was a loud "Squawkkkk." Mickey and I looked at each other in disbelief. Then we started laughing.

"Can't you just see something like this happening back home?" I said. "It's not exactly like Kentucky Fried. But it will be fresh."

"Good thing you didn't order steak!" Mickey remarked.

About thirty minutes later we had fresh fried chicken Chinese style!

So often it happened that just when our struggles with the film studio were getting us down, we found ourselves the recipients of their unusual efforts to please us. We had to remind ourselves not to let the filming problems discolor our overall view of our hosts.

Sunday night, November 18, with just three weeks to go, I lay awake while others were snoring around me, and talked into my recorder:

> I suppose I'm just like anybody else. . . . I have my moments of doubt—what in the world am I doing here? All the things I espouse, are they only fancy phrases, or do I really believe all

the things I talk about? . . . sometimes you wonder if the cost is too great. But I don't think so; not on this. . . . There's doubts and fears, but you've gotta dismiss 'em. Some mornings I wake up and wonder if anyone really cares. But I have to put that aside. I know a lot of people are praying. . . .

After supper on Wednesday night, November 21, Grace said, "We have a treat in store for you now. You have been asking if you could visit a church, so tonight we are going to take you to one."

The drive to Changsha, a large city in the southern province of Hunan, took almost half an hour. At dark we stopped in front of a gate in a high brick wall. Through the iron gate we could see a small brick church building inside. Mr. Wong got out and opened the gate, and drove us in.

A meeting was in session. Since we were permitted to film our visit, Mickey and a couple of cameramen had gone before us to set up the lights and position the cameras; seeing us drive up, Mickey came outside.

"You're going to be absolutely amazed," he told me.

Through large doors we passed into a small foyer. To the left and right were stairs leading to the sanctuary. Once inside, I walked down to about the fifth row and took a seat.

At the front, the pastor, whom I guessed to be about sixty-five-years old, continued speaking as Grace and I filed in. As I learned later, he was instructing new converts in the Christian faith in preparation for their baptism. The people numbered about forty-five in all; the youngest were in their early twenties and the eldest looked to be about seventy-five. Grace and I sat on the women's side.

Other than the large cross on the front of the plain pulpit, the worship hall had no ornamentation. The pastor wore the same blue coat and pants that most of the people wore.

About halfway through his lesson the lights went out. But that bothered no one. They seemed to be accustomed to that, for in a few seconds several candles were lit.

The pastor taught from his open Bible, but no one else had a Bible. He was teaching, not preaching. His manner was earnest, serious, though at times he would arouse a ripple of laughter from among his hearers. At the end, he had the congregation stand. Then he looked up, closed his eyes, and led the congregation in a prayer in unison. I later learned that they were praying the Lord's Prayer.

Afterward, he invited us to join the people for some tea and small cakes, apples, and tangerines. Feeling so grateful to be among these believers, I reached out my hand to shake theirs and most everyone grasped my hand with both of theirs, and smiled warmly.

Mr. Lee, the pastor, explained that these people were undergoing a nine-month instruction period to see if they were worthy to be baptized and recognized as a part of the church. The congregation totaled some 600 members, he said.

Before the Communists came to power in 1949, Buddhism was the dominant religion in China. Ostensibly, religion is guaranteed by the constitution, which states: "Citizens of the People's Republic of China enjoy freedom of religious belief. No state organ, public organization, or individual may compel citizens to believe in, or not to believe in, any religion."[*] I was curious to know how much freedom the church now enjoys and how churches go about spreading the gospel.

"Do you advertise in the papers?" I asked the pastor. "How do you get people to come to church?"

"We depend on the Holy Spirit," he replied. "That allows the Spirit to work."

"Do you need Bibles?"

"Not really. The government allowed one million Bibles to be printed this year, and we are able to get Bibles."

Evidently the church in China is allowed certain freedoms. New congregations are being formed every week say reports printed in the United States in 1985 and, according to one article I've read since coming home, something like 1800 churches have been reopened there in the last six years. The church is growing and reaching out; of that we were witnesses.

---

[*] *Life in Modern China*, China Spotlight Series, p. 76.

"In four years the number of Christians has grown from nine hundred thousand to three million," Pastor Lee said.

Later, when I talked with David Aikman about this, he said that that figure is far too low. "The government wants the people to believe there are only three million Christians in China, but the true figure is closer to thirty million." (Some estimate there are 50 million Christians.) That sounds like a lot. But in fact it would be only 2 or 3 percent of China's population.

Coming from the church meeting I asked one staff member of China Sports what she thought about what she had seen. "It all makes sense now," she said. "I had never known what the church believed until tonight."

Three members of the film crew who were there that night were Muslims. One of them, from then on, would usually greet me by making the sign of the cross and then giving me a "thumbs up," saying "Oh—Kay!"

If the number of Christians is 30 million, I do not know how many Chinese are atheists. But that same week I had a long talk with one of their number.

His name also was Lee, one of the more familiar family names in China. He and I had talked briefly for two days. He spoke English quite well, having studied it ten years in his job as a translator for the government. He was a bright man. He wanted to talk about philosophy and history and would refer to T. S. Eliot, Faulkner, and other literary figures. He was quite conversant with them—far more than I was.

Then one evening he knocked on my door and came in while I was listening to shortwave. Polite and eager to question what he heard, he sat down and we conversed long into the night.

I asked him if he would like to come to America some day.

"Oh, no," he said, "maybe Africa." I had heard more than one Chinese express the same idea.

"America is a very great country," he said. "We can learn much from you."

Thanking him, I said that I felt we could also learn a great deal from China.

But he said, "No, no, no. America is great in music, art, po-
etry, literature, philosophy, and science. Why is this? Your
country is only a little over two hundred years old. We are
over seven thousand years old."

I thought for a moment. I guess I have never had to explain
why. I agree that "We hold these truths to be self-evident.
. . ."

Reaching over to one of my bags, I felt in one of the com-
partments and brought out a quarter in American money.
Showing it to him I asked what words he found on the coin.

"In God we trust."

I said that if there is any one factor that makes America
great, it is this.

"Our country's founding fathers got on their knees and
dedicated our country to the living God and His Son Jesus
Christ. Our land was to be a place where we could worship
openly, without fear, and have the freedom to pursue the
dreams of our hearts. That's what has made America so
strong. Every day untold millions of Americans pray, 'This
day, Almighty God, I put my trust in you.'"

"Well, I don't know," he said. "I don't believe in God."

He shrugged off the religious ways of many Chinese by
calling their beliefs superstition. He seemed totally convinced
of the supremacy of science.

"The theory of medicine, such as acupuncture, cannot be
fully explained now," he told me. "But I think that after several years, science will explain it."

"What if science were to say God is real?" I asked.

"No scientist could say that," he replied.

"But many scientists are saying it."

"I've never heard of it. I've never seen any evidence of
that."

"If I send you evidence, what will you say then?"

"Give me that evidence," he demanded.

"I don't have it with me right this minute," I told him. "But
I will definitely send it to you, because many of the top scientists in the world believe in God."

He did not deny that, but explained that they were "believers" because of the way they were taught when young, and because at present, science cannot explain some things.

"After long years, science will explain it. That's my point."

We talked for a while about the expanse of the universe. "God has come to this planet," I said. "Jesus, the Son of God, was raised from the dead. That's an indisputable fact."

"In China there is some report of dead men coming to life again," he said.

"Yes, a lot of people will die for ten minutes or thirty minutes, and then be revived."

"No," he said, "that's not what I mean. According to a report from the period of the Han dynasty, which was about two thousand years ago, a maiden died and was placed in a tomb. After several hundred years they dug up the tomb of the lady and she came back to life."

"Wow."

"But I can't believe it," he said.

"No. But in the case of Jesus Christ, so many people actually saw Him raised up and go into the heavens."

Mr. Lee had evidently done a lot of thinking about life, and he told me that he did not believe in any life beyond the grave. I felt sorry for this bright young man, and he was probably disappointed in finally finding an American with whom to talk, and discovering that I was "superstitious."

"I just believe in myself," he said. "I'm happy; everything is going fine for me."

"For thirty-eight years the same thing could be said of me. I knew there was a God, but I really didn't believe in Him."

He looked at me: "You didn't believe?"

"No. But three years ago I turned to Him, and ever since, I've never known such happiness in my life. Ten years from now, or twenty years from now, something might happen in your life and you will want God. If you just utter a prayer and say 'O God, help me,' He is ready to hear you and deliver you."

Mr. Lee said he didn't think he would ever do that, but I told him, "Some people say there is no moon, but that doesn't mean the moon is any less real. It's the same way with God. You cannot be sure that life will continue as it is today—and there is a life beyond this life, and a God who will hold us accountable for the way we have lived."

The hour was late and Mr. Lee excused himself. I never saw him again. But I've thought of him many times since then and hope to meet him again one day. He made me think about our own destiny as a nation. In China, they speak of looking sixty years ahead—and say that their children will be prosperous then. I wonder how many Americans are thinking even one year ahead. We had better look ahead and devote our thinking to a lot more important things in life than who is going to win the NFL championship next year, or what television program we're going to watch, or what exotic vacation spot we can go to. We had better live up to the motto on our money.

What we have in the United States is an oasis in the middle of a desert. Our complacency is slowly drying up our unique place in the sun.

We mustn't allow ourselves to sink into self-centeredness. Everyone can do something unique; every person has a gift to give the world. I thought about the fact that there are so many Mr. Lees in the world who would love to have the opportunity to live just one day in our good old USA and I found myself praying, "Please, dear God, don't turn Your face away from America."

17

The Lonely Runner

Observing the masses moving about their daily routine in such a regimented manner, I found myself speculating that perhaps years of education and a gradual relaxing of the external controls would be necessary before the Chinese could be ready to practice democracy. For now the people most likely need the structure that is provided them in their society. I never would have had such a thought from afar; I had to see China to believe it.

During the Cultural Revolution, which rocked the nation from 1965 to 1975, great numbers of intellectuals and professional people were sent into the country to relearn the life of the peasant. Grace, though she is a university graduate, worked for four years learning to grow cotton. This isn't necessarily bad. I think that if a real disaster hit our country a lot of people would starve because they don't know how to feed themselves or make their own clothes or build any kind of shelter.

Books were burned by the Red Guards, and family pictures of the most innocent nature were destroyed, so that the people could be reeducated. The only form of "entertainment" at that time was the daily readings from Chairman Mao that were broadcast several times a day to the people. One member of China Sports, in telling me about that time, wondered aloud that the people allowed themselves to be so completely dominated by so few. Of course, as the opportunity came, many of the best and brightest of the Chinese fled the country. I was told that today, with much freer access to information through books and periodicals, the people are somewhat confused by what they had drummed into them during the more rigid years just past under Communism. That revolution has left severe emotional scars on the people.

Remnants of the Cultural Revolution linger on in modern China. In the country, they are awakened every morning with announcements and news over the loudspeakers. In true Pavlovian style, a dinner bell rings, directing the people: "Now you will eat." And more loudspeakers in the fields tell them when they may take a break. But you don't see guards overseeing their work. Apparently the people have submitted to their strict way of life much like children who obey their elders. The people work long and hard days, doing backbreaking chores; they are disciplined beyond all imagination.

The Communist government has begun to allow some forms of free enterprise. An individual may keep what he makes from selling some of his chickens or eggs or produce, after he has filled his quota. We met one villager who operated a sort of "home restaurant"; people go to his home to eat his cooking and we were told that he makes about 12,000 yuan a year, roughly $4,000, in this way. He is considered very wealthy. The "rat man" whom we met earlier makes about 20,000 yuan a year.

Every morning when I awoke I wondered what new surprises awaited us.

On November 22, eighteen days away from the finish, I should have stayed in bed. At mid-morning, as I was making good time and enjoying running in the warm sunshine, word came down that the Beijing Film Studio would provide no more film for the run. This shocked me because only the day before, a high official of China Sports had said to me, "The run is proceeding very well." He must have known that they were going to stop providing film, but he couldn't bear to be open with me.

That evening I discovered why. Carol told me that the payment due a week earlier had not been made. We had raised only half the amount required and they had decided to send nothing until all $50,000 was in hand. I could see their reasoning. But it was a mistake.

"The Chinese don't think like we think," I told her. "Tell Tyler to wire the money today. We've got to have it or we'll not be able to film the finish. The rest of the money will come in."

I was spent—emotionally exhausted—and now this! At times, black depression would engulf me. I couldn't stand having anybody with me. The slurping of the people at meals irritated me. I even hated the crowds. My only consolation during this time came through running. I *knew* these "black" intervals could not last forever, just as I *knew* that somehow the money we needed would be supplied. All I could do was run through to the sunshine.

Adding to my misery was the fact that virtually all the body fat on my hips had disappeared. At nights, I tossed and turned on the hard beds and could not find sleep.

One day, passing a peasant's home, I paused to greet the family who lived there. They invited me in for tea, and I accepted it, sitting down on a wooden chair in the middle of the room. The woman served tea and Mickey tried not to interrupt my rest—all the while training a hand-held camera on the interior of the home. My back was killing me, so I laid my head down on their table and rested, just to stretch my backbone—it felt as if I had been beating it with a sledgehammer all day. In a minute I was asleep, and arose from there refreshed for more running.

During the run my feet swelled, as they have done on every other ultradistance run, and to make room for my swollen feet, I slit the sides of my shoes. The Chinese thought this strange and it would have made a corporate shoe executive cringe with dismay to see how I "air-conditioned" their product for the long haul.

On November 27 something happened to cheer all of us—especially Mickey. It was his son Christopher's first birthday. At dinner that night, Grace surprised us by bringing a beautifully decorated cake to our table, with one tall lighted candle standing in the center. Mickey would much rather have been home, and the revelry around that table was not without tears—but it was one of those happy times of rejoicing in our common ties with our fellowman. The Chinese sang "Happy Birthday, Christopher" to Mickey!

Grace was doing everything she could to stuff me with potatoes now; and occasionally we had butter. I couldn't eat much else. It was the same problem—if I couldn't get it past my nose, I didn't trust it in my stomach. There was the day they served us gelatinous eggs prepared in such a way that they resembled green mucus.

In those lean days Mickey and I got by with the aid of a "care package" from home. Lois and Anna had sent some peanut butter and a box of oatmeal cookies, and after an impossibly long journey, they finally arrived one evening. Mickey and I were like kids on Christmas morning, tearing into the contents of that package.

Two nights later, the only word I could think of to describe the supper offered to us was *pathetic*. I could not eat it. Again, it was Peter Pan to the rescue! I got by eating peanut butter on some slices of bread and drinking my fill of *moli hwa cha*. That night we were at the border of Hunan and Guangdong provinces in a very poor village.

Pressing toward the goal, I now pictured Guangzhou, my final destination, out there ahead of me in the distance much as I had visualized the Rock of Gibraltar during the last weeks of the Europe run. Each day I was drawing that much closer to Guangzhou.

Most mornings I awakened and thought that rigor mortis had done its work. I was stiff. Some days they almost had to cart me to the starting point and set me on the road. I really wondered if I could walk, let alone run the daily goals they had for me. But, beginning with a walk of about four kilometers, and then a shuffle, I would ease into the day's run.

The only way I could keep going was by breaking the day into segments. I would divide the morning into four hours and then break the hours into quarter hours. When it was really tough going, I would even break the time into five-minute parts. I would work through each segment, put it behind me, and go on to the next one. I would not allow myself to think of how far I had been or how far I had to go.

Running gives me a lot of time to think. I can go on effortlessly as long as my mind has something to focus on. But after almost forty days on the road, I began to play the same mental tapes over again. That's a part of the anguish of the long-distance runner. You just keep going, and you're glad for any and every surprise that snaps you momentarily out of your boredom. But a lot of the time you just keep running and hurting.

As I kept clicking off the kilometers I was reminded of my daddy's skillful way of splitting and riling the white oak canes for the baskets he made so well. People recognized him as one of the best basket makers in Kentucky. He demonstrated his craft at the Mammoth Cave National Park, one of the largest tourist attractions in Kentucky; folks would come from far and near to buy his baskets.

I used to watch him. So many times when I thought he surely could not split the oak strips any thinner, he would run his knife down through a strip and out would come a new one. Running now for almost seven weeks, I felt every fiber of my being was being peeled back just like that white oak. I wondered that there was any more I could give, any more of "me" left. Each day demanded every bit of strength and persistence I had, and when I thought I could not go another mile, I somehow found new reserves . . . and the ability to go on.

I identified with Alice in Wonderland when the Mad Hatter asked her who she was. She answered: "I don't know. I've changed so many times since this morning."

The experience of a long-distance run always brings me into touch with my deeper subconscious. Once again running became like dreaming—events of my past would open to me, people I hadn't seen in years flashed before my mind's eye, songs and Scriptures would come to me in new kaleidoscopic patterns and form the creative seeds of new thinking. These new thoughts would sometimes entertain my mind for several miles; at such times I felt as though I could run forever. Body, mind, and spirit were all in one accord. Effortlessly I went, the miles melting away. It was a beautiful, euphoric feeling. *How wondrously and marvelously I am made,* I thought.

Sometimes the simplest things helped me keep going. In Hunan province I ran for part of a morning beside a rampaging river, and I imagined myself drawing strength from this white water show of energy.

Meeting the people took my mind off myself and my aching muscles. At times I felt I could not go on, and then I would turn a corner and see someone interesting. One day it was at an elementary school. We stopped to visit and film the children and what impressed me was the strict discipline of the classrooms. All the teachers were males and they each had charge of two classrooms of children, ages six through eight. Each teacher carried a long stick and when he would leave one classroom to go across a dirt path into the other room, the children did not make one peep. Their heads were down and they were hard at work with their lessons. It reminded me of the discipline in American schools years ago.

That evening a father and his two little girls, ten and eight years of age, were among the throng lining the road in the town where we were to stay. I learned that they had skipped school that day and had waited five hours for our arrival.

Their special presents were lovely bouquets of fresh flowers; but that was not all. They also sang a song for me, which I've since had translated. (The rhododendron is a small bird.)

> Small rhododendron, we ask you to sing a song.
> Come everyone, come,
> Let's listen to your song!
> Gu, gu. Gu, gu.
> This really makes us happy.
> Gu, gu. Gu, gu.

The people I met were to my psyche what a drink of water was to the body. I would wonder what lay ahead and the mystery of it pulled me forward. And each day as I got my muscles warmed up, I only knew one thing: *Forward!*

As the run neared its climax, every morning I thought—*As long as I can stand, I will never give up. I know I can hang on for eighteen days. I know I can. And this will be a reality . . . I will have achieved my goal in this, the hardest race of my life.*

I had thought this China run would be easier than it turned out to be. In my mind I had envisioned only the road and I had confidence that I could run the distance. I just thought, *How fascinating to do it in China!* But as I was finding out, China was different, very different from any other place I had ever run.

For one thing, the living conditions proved to be more primitive than any I had ever experienced. The Chinese knew they were offering me crude accommodations, and they apologized regularly for "poor conditions." We had no heat in our rooms most of the way, and hot water and bathing were occasional luxuries. In many places where we stayed, the hot water was turned off about 10:00 P.M., and sometime later in the night the water was completely shut off.

The dust often caked on my skin and choked up my breathing. With few exceptions, I only saw a toilet when we stayed in the occasional international-style hotels.

As simple a thing as making a telephone call presented formidable obstacles. Usually I had to wait twelve hours after placing a call for it to get through to the United States.

Much of the time I never quite knew where I was running in a given day. The provincial police routed us through villages and over trails, and I did not always know how many kilometers I would be running.

Also, the financial problems were astounding. Many days we absolutely did not know if the run might be stopped or the filming canceled because of failure of funds.

The food was 1000 percent different from anything I had known before. I don't consider myself a finicky eater—it's just that the normal, everyday fare of the Chinese did not look appetizing or smell appealing to me. (Of course, I realize our food might not appeal to them either. It's all what you're used to.) Rare were the times when I encountered extremes, like snake or monkey brain. It was just that I could not make a meal out of their regular fare. I tried the fish and the tofu, but I couldn't bring myself to eat much of it. And the exceptional greasiness of the meat dishes turned me away from them. Thank goodness for potatoes, eggs, mineral water, and tea!

The constant presence of police was something I had never encountered; they were always around me. I was pulled and shoved when the people crowded around me while running, and though I knew they were doing it for my protection, I never got used to it.

We were cut off from the rest of the world, isolated from a ready source of news of our families and about what was going on in general. This did strange things to our morale, so much so that sometimes I convinced myself that everyone had abandoned us. Thankfully, those notions didn't last long, and I had only to look inward for the real truth—I had *chosen* this long road and all the isolation it entailed.

The greatest difference between this run and any other, I suppose, lay in the ambitious film project. I had never tried such a thing, and I'm sure it's evident by now that the complexities of such an endeavor almost proved our undoing time after time. Working out the frustrations and hostilities in dealing with the film crew seemed to be good for something, however; it moved me on down the road!

Oddly enough, it was the Chinese who provided my biggest incentive to keep going. I saw how the people worked, and I knew that if they could do that day after day, I could keep running. In Hunan province, where a stretch of some 105 kilometers of road was being widened, I must have seen 50,000 people—men, women, and children—hauling dirt. I think they were all called out to the job by the provincial governor. They carried dirt in two wicker baskets extended from bamboo poles on their shoulders, toiling obediently, and as far as I could tell, without complaining.

They would load their baskets with soil and then wait in line to have their load weighed—each basket could hold about thirty pounds—and then go and dump it at the road site. Then they would repeat it all over again, going back for who knows how many more loads.

Seeing how little they had, and how hard they have to work, how could I complain about my problems?

Our first night in Guangdong province, November 30, we were lodged in a "hotel" high on the side of the mountain. We must have ascended steps on a fifty-degree angle to reach the place. But we forgot all about the tough climb when we sat down to the most delicious meal we had eaten in a long while. Finally, we thought, we had reached Cantonese country! The meals would be better, we hoped. But we hoped in vain. Soon I was to learn that it was to be a very long ten days before the finish, in so far as the food was concerned. I mean we were treated to real delicacies—like snake, monkey brain, cat, and *gol roe.*

One night Mickey and I wandered into an inn in southern Hunan province, looking for some *moli hwa cha.* But the place smelled odd. It wasn't long before we discovered that the dogs that were caged along one wall were the *gol roe* being served from the kitchen. I almost gagged and had to exit the place in a hurry.

Though our rooms were not heated, I did have a surprise. Grace told me that the people, knowing I was coming, had installed a hot water heater in the room for my bath. I was later to find out that it had only a one-gallon capacity—so, my hot shower was over with rather quickly. We were still encountering dust on the road and the water from my shower turned black when I rinsed off.

The next two days took us through the highest mountains we were to encounter in China, and also the most breathtakingly beautiful. No developments or ski lifts were there to mar the natural beauty. The narrow road made its way treacherously through a high pass. On one side at times the mountain dropped sharply a thousand or two thousand feet, and guardrails were nonexistent! I was never so frightened in all my life nor have I ever been so thankful to have any part of a run behind me as that stretch of road.

Pausing to assess the damages I had received on the run to this point, I began to wonder about my feet. My right foot had swelled more than on previous runs, and bruises discolored the top of the foot. Stress fracture, I imagined. My knees throbbed at the end of each day, and my legs had long since become rubbery. But my feet were what screamed out at night. There *is* such a thing as "barking dogs"!

Yet I was pleased with my level of fitness at this point on the run. My weight was 128 and my resting pulse was consistently in the low 40s. And I was running strongly, once my muscles warmed up each morning.

There is no calamity greater than lavish
desires.
—La Tzu

18

"It's a Miracle"

We were to have one more battle in our war with the Beijing Film Studio, and it erupted on Saturday, December 8, two days before the run was to become history. As usual, Mr. Du was at the center of it and came near to making a calamity of the film project.

That Saturday began innocently enough. China Sports had housed Mickey and me in an absolutely wonderful hotel and I slept like a baby on a real mattress with a real pillow—the first I had seen since Wuhan. We had arrived the night before, smelling like a couple of animals, to find reserved for us a suite of clean, airy bedrooms opening off a spacious area that was large enough to double as a reception room. I had almost forgotten the luxury of squishing my bare feet into cushiony carpet.

The view out our windows was spellbinding. In

the distance we could see the mountain range we had traversed. Spreading out in the immediate foreground below the hills were great expanses of rice paddies, citrus groves, verdant vegetation, all bathed in the early morning sun. It was postcard-China time!

But at this stage of the run I didn't feel like taking the time to smell the flowers. Like a horse returning to food and rest after a day on the trail, I was smelling the barn. So that day I started down the road at 7:30 A.M. About an hour later, Mickey called for me to run through a field where a peasant was plowing behind a water buffalo.

"That'll make a great shot," he said.

Once I reached the farmer I yelled to Mickey that I was going to see if the man would allow me to plow a little, and he did. I figured plowing is like anything else; if you've done it before—albeit never behind a water buffalo—you still know how. I took the reins and for a few minutes I was transported in my thoughts back home to Kentucky. I plowed a few yards while Mickey and Mrs. Shr recorded it all on film. That was enough to remind me what hard work plowing is.

But Mickey was not too happy. He thought the camera was malfunctioning. He could tell by the sound it was making that something had gone awry. Mrs. Shr, his most reliable camera operator, handed the camera to Mickey and when he tested it he became all the more sure that the machine was defective.

Then the truth came out. Mr. Du had taken the functioning camera and had gone twenty kilometers down the road ahead of us. By the time Mickey found this out, I had resumed my running. But as soon as his vehicle caught up with me I could see Mickey was very upset.

"Stan, you're not going to believe this," he yelled as he jumped out of the car, waving his arms.

"What's wrong?"

"We're shooting film with a camera that doesn't work;

there's something wrong with the film gate. And Mr. Du has disappeared with the good camera."

Mr. Du had been successful a lot of the time in disguising his ineptness by acting as if he did not understand what Mickey had told him to do. But we had concluded that probably his real problem was jealousy of Mrs. Shr. She spoke and read English and had a solid documentary background being a filmmaker with China's Scientific Film Studio. She was easily the most proficient of the camera crew—Mickey thought she was one of the best he had ever worked with anywhere. Also, Du continued to resent Mickey's know-how, so he had persisted in playing the power game. He could commandeer a driver when he wanted to, and that is what he had done that morning.

The day was ideal for running, but I called off any further work until Mr. Du showed up—despite knowing that probably two hours would be lost in clearing up this problem. I was thinking now of the finish of the run. By this time, according to Mickey's daily calculations, we had shot over 90,000 feet of film and we did not need very much more in the way of scenery shots or on-camera conversations. But we would have to be assured that the cameras were working properly for shooting the finish in Guangzhou. We would only have one chance.

We had not waited long before a car appeared in the distance. It was Mr. Du. Mickey did the talking, with Grace continuing to translate. The frustrating part was knowing that Du was probably not understanding very much of what Mickey was saying.

Mickey turned and headed for the *da puncha* for our tape recorders, and I think I blew my stack at Mr. Du about that time. His behavior was a breach of contract as far as I was concerned. There was no financial risk involved for Du; he was only interested in "putting film into the can." Mickey and I, on the other hand, had our financial backers to worry about. We had a heavy responsibility to these investors who were entitled to the best film we could put together. It turned out that Du had used up about 2,000 feet of film shooting a basketball game that had nothing to do with our film.

In the process of our clearing up this latest headache, someone said to me: "We must work together in a spirit of unity and cooperation." I couldn't agree more; that's what we had wanted all along. But the sentiment sounded a little empty with only two and a half days left.

By lunchtime I had defused somewhat. I was calm enough to indicate to the crew that the run would resume at 2:30 and that if all of them—including Mr. Du—were not on the road then, I would consider it a final breach of contract.

At the appointed hour I started running, and once again a major crisis passed.

The filmmaking part of this venture continued to prove equally as challenging as running the daily distance. Looking back now, I could see how green I was when it came to understanding filmmaking. And I hadn't realized how important titles, credits, and responsibilities were for the crew. I had trusted the studio and had assumed that they knew how to do a film of the kind I envisioned. And in trusting them, I had placed Mickey at a gigantic handicap.

Much as I would like the film to be well-received by the critics, what concerned me more was what my own family would think of it. Sometimes while Mickey would be shooting a scene or interviewing me on camera, I would ask myself, *What will my son see in this? How will he view it? Will he say, "Yeah, that's my dad"? Will he see a side of me that sets goals and strives for achievement? Will Dad be believable to him? And will it inspire him to strive for excellence, to test the limits?*

And I wondered if my Michelle and Jennifer will benefit from what they see. I hope they will. I pray they will. I want them to face life with courage and not be afraid of getting a blackened eye. This film would be a kind of legacy to leave with them, of Dad in China doing one small thing in an effort to bring about greater friendship and more understanding between nations.

A year after graduating from Western Kentucky University in 1966, I had taken a teaching job on the south side of Jacksonville, Florida, at Englewood High School. Along with teaching psychology, I coached the cross-country and track teams, and one of my charges that year was John Hedquist. I never thought I would see young John again when I moved our family to Savannah, Georgia, two years later.

But in the summer of '84 I unexpectedly met John again. I had been invited to the Perimeter Presbyterian Church in Atlanta to take part in a program on the life of the runner Eric Liddell. It was at that difficult "barbecue" stage of my fundraising efforts for the China run. After speaking, I was on my way out when a tall, brown-haired man came running after me, calling, "Coach Cottrell." It was John. I remember how I had almost not accepted the invitation to speak at that church that day. But it turned out to be one of those divine appointments. John immediately became an enthusiast for the China run.

Now, no more than a half-hour after we had settled the dispute over the film, and while we had stopped to shoot a scene, Kevin drove up and out jumped John!

Carol had told me he was coming to run with me into Guangzhou. I don't think I was ever so glad to see anybody in all my life. John and I hugged each other, and then I introduced him to our seasoned "road crew." He had kept up his running and was "hot to trot" with me; so we broke into a run, talking all the way. Soon I had forgotten all the troubles of the morning.

After lunch we made good progress for the remainder of Day 51. My heart was really pumping the adrenaline now, spurred on by John's companionship, for I didn't really feel that well. I had a deep chest cold. My vitamins were all gone and my nerves were shot. My body had long before stopped asking what I was trying to do, and my brain had gone to rest saying, "You're insane!"

Just one more week and you'll be home, I told myself.

On my final phone call home before the finish, I asked Carol to book me on a flight to Hong Kong on December 11, and from there home. Anna and Lois and little Christopher were arriving on Monday (December 10), and Kevin and Anna wanted me to stay in China for a few days, but I was determined to head for home. How sweet to contemplate returning to the good ol' USA. Flights from Guangzhou to Hong Kong had to be reserved a week in advance, so heavy is the flow of passengers between those two cities.

Carol told me that Jennifer had finally received a letter I had written and had read it to her class at school. I could see my Jenny reading that letter, probably stumbling over the Chinese words, and the mere thought of it brought tears to my eyes.

I had some mail to read myself. That afternoon Kevin brought in a package Carol had told me was coming. It was a cardboard box containing 500 letters and cards from schoolchildren in the Garrett Middle School in Austell, Georgia. John and I opened and read them one by one while Kevin looked over my shoulder.

Some of them said, "Go, Stan, go." Or, "Don't give up!" I laughed at some of the pictures they drew, and got a lump in my throat too. How could I give up, with such nice friends encouraging me?

"So many say they are praying for you," Kevin commented.

He also noticed that one letter referred to a proverb. He seemed curious when I opened my study Bible and turned to Proverbs. I pointed to a verse and asked him to read it.

"A soft answer turneth away wrath: but grievous words stir up anger. . . . In the house of the righteous is much treasure: but in the revenues of the wicked is trouble" (15:1, 6).

"Very good!" he said.

We read some more, as Kevin's interest was aroused.

"Would you accept my Bible as a gift?" I asked him.

"Why yes. Thank you very much."

Kevin stayed in my room long enough to brief me on the schedule China Sports had arranged for the conclusion of the run on Monday.

"Many plans have been made to show you the appreciation of the Chinese people for The Great Friendship Run," Kevin said.

More good things continued.

John opened one of his bags and pulled out apple juice, peanut butter, and Snickers bars. How I had wished for some of this earlier!

"How about a Fig Newton?" he said.

"Why not?" I responded. "Make it two—I feel like splurging."

When John opened his briefcase, Kevin saw an audiocassette there, one that contained worship and praise songs. Already, seeing Kevin's spiritual hunger, John had been a bit amazed, but when Kevin asked if he could listen to that cassette the following day, he was almost stunned.

"Of course," John said.

John and I talked into the night. He felt overwhelmed at being in China and having the opportunity to let his light shine there. Finally, after more prayer, we turned in.

Sunday I ran like a gazelle—58 kilometers, my last full day of running. Sinewy and leathered by the elements, a mere feather at 130 pounds, I ran shirtless that day. It was marvelous.

We were at a picturesque hotel by three o'clock with but 23 kilometers—some 15 miles—to go to the finish.

That day Grace accompanied Mickey and Mr. Du into Guangzhou, to look at the route I would be running on the final day. It would be crucial to locate the cameras at strategic points along the route. After Du's actions the previous day, hard feelings still hung on. Grace had been embarrassed for

Du, and Mickey had lost all respect for him. This didn't make their work that day any easier.

Mickey's frustrations continued to mount as they traveled through downtown Guangzhou. They had no idea where the people were likely to be gathered to observe the run. And going in on a Sunday didn't help.

Mickey asked how the people would know that I would be finishing the run. Grace told him that the television stations would announce the run. But she was not sure if they would tell the people the exact route and schedule.

That night Mickey attended a meeting of the Beijing Film Studio and again tried to raise the question about how we could be assured of the "people factor."

"You don't want to just shoot Stan running all by himself amidst the cars and bicycles. You want people along the route. Can we print up some leaflets and distribute them beforehand?"

"Don't worry," he was told. "Everything is taken care of." His words had fallen on deaf ears.

After the run on Sunday, once we arrived in our hotel room, I shed my sweaty shoes, revealing blood-soaked socks and several black toes. This startled John.

"It's all in a day's running," I said, being a little too nonchalant. All day I had run under a very warm sun, with only a lunch break. Having someone to run with, and knowing that soon the run would be over, I didn't want to stop running that day. I never removed my shoes at all. Blisters on top of blisters had burst and formed callouses. Yet I had truthfully felt no pain. I was "smelling the barn."

Monday morning, December 10, I dressed with the finish in mind. I would be carrying a small Chinese flag and a small United States flag that day, so I wore colors to match—white shorts with a red stripe, and a red shirt, with the predominantly blue Salvation Army flag knotted about my neck.

At breakfast we encountered more Caucasians than we had seen since leaving the Great Wall. One of a sizable group of touring Australians came to our table and said, "You're the runner, aren't you?"

"Yes, sir, I am."

"We've read about you in the papers. I think it's absolutely a lovely thing you're doing."

A woman in the group who was wearing a kangaroo pin on her blouse removed it and pinned it to my warm-up suit.

"I want you to have this as a token of good cheer from Australia," she said. We posed for pictures with these folks, and I wanted to stay and talk with them. Their distinctive accent engaged my attention; Mickey and I were hungry to hear more English, even if it did have an Aussie flavor! But we had work to do—if you want to call it that. This final 23 kilometers would be more play than work.

I had not slept much the night before, so anxious was I to finish. At about 8:30 our gypsy wagon drove us the 5 kilometers to the beginning point.

It was cool and sunny, and I was froggy, wound up tighter than a tent rope. The route took me from the suburbs toward the heart of the city on a highway that began to resemble an expressway in America. After only forty-five minutes I had already gotten ahead of schedule, so we took a rest stop alongside the highway. John and I had fun handing out peppermint candy and gum and Fig Newtons to children who gathered around the vehicles.

When we resumed the run over the multi-laned road, I continued running to the far right, well shielded by the police vehicles and the China Sports Service Company cars. I held the flags and waved to passersby, many of whom honked and waved back. But Mickey's suspicions appeared to be confirmed. There were no crowds along the way. Not that I minded. We had been thronged by China's masses for most of the way, and I had wished for more space. In Guangzhou, amid mid-morning traffic, I had that. But without people along the route, our attempt to create a visual climax for the film fizzled.

Once during that day, Mr. Wong drove up beside me to

allow Kevin to call out some instructions about the finish. I thought at first that I was hearing things. In the car Kevin and Mr. Wong had the volume on their cassette player turned way up and the sounds of a familiar song wafted across to me:

> Open my eyes, Lord,
> I want to see Jesus,
> To reach out and touch Him,
> and say that I love Him. . . .*

Wow!

Leaving the highway to enter the downtown streets, we passed a large square where crowds were assembled. Some in their cars honked their horns at us. *They know!* I told myself. *They know that the run is almost completed.* The thought buoyed my spirits even more. From the curb, people waved and smiled broadly. Following my police escorts down a main street, I did not know how much farther I had to go. I was running easily, greeting occasional bystanders with a *"Ni hau"* and watching which way the escorts were leading me.

Then we turned a corner. A few blocks ahead of me the street emptied onto a rather long, straight, two-laned bridge, leading directly to an ultramodern building that loomed large against the distant horizon. I knew instantly that this was the White Swan Hotel. I had the finish in sight!

In moments I caught up with our entourage, except for the film trucks, which proceeded on across the bridge. All the rest had stopped at the foot of the bridge that spanned the last half-mile.

As I approached the near end of the bridge, a policeman told me: "You'll run this alone." And in a few short steps, I was on the bridge, a warm sun beaming down on me as though my heavenly Father were giving me His blessing. Ahead of me in the hazy urban air stood the hotel.

At first I paced across the bridge briskly. But then I thought: *Slow down. Savor this brief moment.* Deliberately, I slowed my pace. I knew that within minutes I would cross the

*OPEN OUR EYES, by Bob Cull © 1976 Maranatha! Music. All rights reserved. International copyright secured. Used by permission only.

finish line and this run would be history. Funny, now I almost felt sad that the run was about to end. I slowed my pace a bit more, relishing these last minutes.

It had not been possible for me to run alone very much on this endeavor. Every time I thought I was all alone, a police car would come in view, or a film truck would come along to monitor my running and get some footage. Now I was indeed all alone with only my thoughts to keep me company.

Pit, pat, pit, pat . . . my shoes struck the pavement.

Pit, pat, pit, pat, pit, pat. Then Bang! Bang! Pow! Pow! Bang! Pow! It startled me at first. What was happening?

Then I caught sight of smoke rising from the entrance to the hotel and knew they were firing the first of 10,000 firecrackers as a part of the welcoming festivities for me at the finish. Actually, the plan called for this to happen just as I crossed the finish line, but when the film trucks reached the middle of the bridge, off they went.

As I neared the finish, I could see about a dozen young Chinese girls dressed alike in tan dresses and waving something in their hands. They lined up on opposite sides of the road, at the end of the bridge, and across the road was stretched a wide red ribbon.

Now across the entrance to the White Swan Hotel I could see a large banner in red and white. It said "Finish of The Great Friendship Run."

The fireworks were spent as I came toward the finish in the quiet morning air. And I was spent too. Only at that time I felt no pain. I was rushing toward the fulfillment of a big dream.

Now I could see that the girls were holding small American and Chinese flags like the ones I held. I could hear cheers and applause. I raised the flags high above my head and raced across the finish line. The time was 10:30 in Guangzhou.

I can't recall exactly what happened next. I know that photographers were shooting picture after picture. And a girl in a beautiful ankle-length dress placed a flowered wreath around my neck. From somewhere out of the crowd John Hedquist rushed to me and gave me a strong embrace.

"You did it, brother . . . You did it!"

All I could do was grin. What a feeling! What a great feeling!

Somewhere in the crowd, my faithful companion Mickey was directing the last bit of filming.

Kevin and Grace and the head of China Sports had arranged a brief program, and one of them began the ceremony by asking for attention over the public-address system.

I recalled earlier finishes.

In 1981, when I reached Louisville and finally achieved a goal that had twice eluded me—running across Kentucky—I almost collapsed from fatigue. I also recalled the joyous finish in San Francisco, completing the run across America. Momma and Carol were there to greet me. Now I wished for them to share this moment with me—and I look forward to the time when the film is finished and at last I will be able to share the ecstasy of those moments with those I love.

In a warm and happy ceremony the head of the China Sports Service Company presented me with a beautiful cloisonné urn. Etched in the base of the urn were these words:

GREAT FRIENDSHIP RUN
BEIJING-GUANGZHOU (2800) KM
Oct. 19 - Dec. 10, 1984
STAN COTTRELL

I was overcome with this gesture. I had never seen a trophy so beautiful, so unique.

Following the ceremony, I was taken to a room they had reserved for me in the hotel. No longer was I looking for hidden microphones or exclaiming over the luxurious carpet. I was elated with the beautiful joy of being one with my Chinese friends. A luncheon at twelve noon—a feast of two suckling pigs—would celebrate our victory. And then again at night we would enjoy one final banquet.

At the evening meal, one official asked how it felt to know my name is spoken on the lips of over 800 million Chinese, and that my name will be written in the history books.

I couldn't answer his question. All I could think of was Mickey's phrase—"Mind-boggling!"

"All I can say," I told the small gathering, "is that when people come together under the banners of love and friendship, something supernatural happens. I feel that what we have accomplished together is another step toward making our planet a better place to live. Our grandchildren's children's children will prosper as a result."

Two people came to mean very much to me during the fifty-three days running through China. On Tuesday, early in the morning, following two grand feasts at the hotel on the day of the finish, these two people went the last distance with me, to the Guangzhou airport.

Grace sat quietly between me and John Hedquist, as Mr. Wong maneuvered the car in the early morning traffic. I felt sad, yet happy. We had traveled together a hundred different times, I think. I had really come to love and respect these two.

Looking about in the car, now filled with luggage, I saw the sack on the seat beside Mr. Wong. In it, I knew, were the jar of Nescafé instant coffee and the creamer that Grace had bought at a Friendship Store in Wuhan. Mr. Wong, who looked for ways to be kind to me, who had helped me into bed many a night when I could hardly walk, and wiped my face at almost every kilometer marker, had added another kindness to the daily rigors of the run. Nearly every morning he would go out to the car and bring that sack in and make me a cup of coffee.

"Here is your coffee, Lao pengyo," he would say with a big smile. He did it in such a way that I could tell he got as big a charge out of it as I did.

Now as I realized he wouldn't be doing that anymore, tears came to my eyes.

"God love your sweet precious gentle heart, Mr. Wong, you

won't be getting me coffee anymore." I was crying like a baby.

"I really will miss you people," I said. I was too choked up with love for them to say any more. Grace put her hand on my hand and patted it. No words were conveyed.

Before, and all through the run, Grace had kept her emotions in check. We had argued and had our confrontations, and we had also laughed. But she had never allowed herself to show any feelings of warmth for this "crazy American." Now it was different. When we reached the airport and John and I were issued boarding passes for our flight, she turned to say good-bye. "You can kiss me," she said. With that she allowed me to give her a tender farewell kiss on the cheek. I hugged both her and Mr. Wong.

Kevin, who had arrived in another car with Mr. Du and Mrs. Kahn, reached out and gave me a hug and said, "We are more than friends; we are now brothers!" With that I wiped the tears from my eyes, struggled to control my emotions, and strode on board.

I sat down in the CAAC plane in a daze, oblivious of the hubbub around me. It had been a miracle run. When *Time*'s David Aikman had interviewed me at the close of the run on Monday, that's all I could say. I was so thankful for the miracle, that we had come and that we had finished.

The following week, *Time* carried a report and picture of me amid flowers and flags, holding the urn aloft. It said:

> As he trotted the final 200 yards along an elevated bridge to Canton's ultramodern White Swan Hotel, the slight, blond runner was greeted by Guangdong province sports officials and svelte Chinese maidens in green cheongsams. But for Georgia's Stan Cottrell, 41, the greatest reward last week was simply finishing the 2,125-mile Great Friendship Run he had begun 53 days earlier from the Great Wall of China, northwest of Peking. "I call this a miracle run," said Cottrell, who held U.S. and Chinese flags as he was presented with a brown cloisonné trophy. "It's a miracle that I'm in China and a miracle that I'm here today."

Epilogue

If someone had told me when I was a schoolboy that this gift of long-distance running would one day bring me before the vice-president of the United States, I would have not believed it. That would be a dream beyond even *my* wildest fantasies. Yet it happened.

Vice-President George Bush had twice encouraged me at critical junctures as I pursued the goal of running in China. And on July 25, 1985, I walked, as if in a dream, into his office in the Executive Office Building, across the street from the White House, to attend a reception in honor of The Great Friendship Run USA.

With me were three *lao pengyos*—Shi Yangjie, Peng Xiangshen, and Li Zhaotai—who had just completed the American counterpart to my run across China, running with me from San Francisco to Washington, D.C. And interpreting for this happy occasion—

187

my close friend, Grace. Also in the room that day were members of my family, three high officials from the Chinese embassy, the director of the President's Council on Physical Fitness and Sports, representatives of the sponsoring companies for the run across America, our support crew, and special guests.

Dressed still in their bright red warm-up suits, the three Chinese runners were clearly the center of Vice-President Bush's attention. Shi, 39, from Changchun, himself a long distance runner, is the head coach for all Jilin province in northeast China, training some of China's outstanding marathoners.

Peng, 32, of Kunming in Yunnan province in the far south, teaches sports and physical education, training youthful athletes in the ways of fitness, teamwork, and sports achievement. He was for three years China's national champion in the 5,000 and 10,000 meters.

Li, 28, of Nanchang in the southeastern province of Jiangxi, works on the assembly line in a tractor manufacturing plant. He is one of his country's three top long-distance runners.

Running across America it had been their turn to taste new foods and wonder what strange experiences awaited them each day. From the time we first arrived in California in early June (I had traveled with Grace and the runners from Beijing), for the next eight weeks, I saw America as I had never seen it, through Chinese eyes. While in China I had realized how rich are her people in their closeness to the land and their tightly knit family life. And I had often thought of how much in material goods they do not have. In America, seeing these fellow humans marvel at so simple a thing as a cold water fountain—unheard of in China—made me realize the value of the common things we so often take for granted.

The first meal in America that Peng, Shi, and Li enjoyed—I think they enjoyed it!—was served them at a Burger King in San Francisco. They ordered a Whopper, french fries and Coca-Cola. We were to enjoy a wide range of delicious food on the trip, including a lot of home-cooked meals, but my Chinese friends adjusted quite well to America's fast-food entrees. At that first meal, all of them marveled that we would have a hot sandwich with a cold drink!

The ice machines in hotels along the way amazed them as did the hay bailer we happened onto while running across Utah. The greatest thing that impressed me was America's enormous friendliness. And this was by no means restricted to the official welcome given us in every state, along with keys to the cities and proclamations of friendship. Families welcomed us to their homes for backyard picnics, and more than once a complete stranger would pick up the tab at a restaurant for our traveling party of ten.

"This is China week in Washington," Vice-President Bush said in greeting us. We knew what he meant, for China's president, Li Shiannian, was that day completing a historic visit in the nation's capital. China flags had adorned the iron fence around the White House during Mr. Li's visit and were on display at several federal buildings. In no way could we have planned for the completion of the run to take place when all Washington, it seemed, was abuzz about China.

"How far have you run?" the vice-president asked.

"Thirty-six hundred miles."

"Really? Where did you start?"

"At city hall in San Francisco," I responded. "On June 10. It took us forty-six days in all."

"And where are you going now?"

"To Atlanta," I said.

"That's good, you'll get to see some of the country. . . . Errr, of course, you've seen quite a bit of the country haven't you?"

That was true. We had crossed fifteen states, averaging eighty to a hundred miles each day. The four of us took turns, each man covering a "short" distance of three to five miles at a time. The Great Friendship Run USA was one giant relay race.

Sponsoring us were Porsche, Inc., American Fitness Centers, of Atlanta, and Ideal food products, of Everett, Washington. The chairman of Porsche, Peter Schutz, provided two 1985 Porsches for our use on the cross-country trip. These were Model 944s, supplied by Porsche Cars North America, Inc., in Reno, Nevada. Don Booker of American Fitness Centers contributed a cash sum toward our expenses and Greg DeBay of Ideal Products, Inc., donated ten cases of their miniaturized nutrition snack, Allfoodtab, and a cash gift.

Dr. Ash Hayes, executive director of the President's Council on Physical Fitness and Sports, had given us the official welcome at the finish of the run that morning at the Capitol. And Senators Wendell Ford of Kentucky and Mack Mattingly of Georgia had taken time off from their heavy schedules to greet the runners while members of the press photographed and taped the ceremony. Receiving Mr. Bush's warm and genuine expression of appreciation that afternoon, I couldn't help recall how Representative "Pat" Swindall of Georgia had completely set aside everything else that morning to greet our Chinese friends, present them with gifts, and pose for pictures with them and all of our party on the steps of the Capitol. Pat is the congressman for our Fifth District back home.

When I told the vice-president how much I appreciated all that his office had done to make the two runs possible, he declined my praise. "I was nothing more than a fly on the wall," he said. Some fly!

"Ruth Graham has spoken to me of you on several occasions," he said. "It is a good thing all of you have done, for international understanding and for fitness."

Assisted by Dr. Hayes, he then presented beautiful commemorative plaques, mounted and framed, to each of us runners. It was quite a thrill, standing between Mr. Bush and Dr. Hayes, for the official photograph. Later, Carol received a well-deserved gesture that was quite a thrill for her. The vice-president invited our entire party to pose for a photograph with him, and he wrapped his arms around Carol just as family would do.

That half-hour with the vice-president, and with my cross-country friends—Shi, Peng, and Li—will forever be etched in my memory. Despite all our differences, the color of our skin, and the language of our tongue, we knew that we all belong to one family. And we knew something else. Friendship comes only at a great price, but it is worth all the effort, all the sweat, all the tears, all the "footwork."

And I knew as I walked hand in hand with Carol down the halls and out the door that day, our dreams really can come true.

UPI / BETTMANN NEWSPHOTOS

Vice-President George Bush greets participants of The Great Friendship Run USA: (*left to right*) Huang Yayan, Peng Xiangshen, Shi Yangjie, Li Zhaotai, Stan Cottrell, Vice-President Bush.